LAST STAGE
WHEN LIFE HAPPENS

THE DIARY OF ELIZABETH ORR

Copyright Notice

Cover Design: Jeremy Prosper
Editing: Joyce Hallenbeck
Publisher: Sun & Moon Publishing/Diana Latteri
sunandmoonpublishing.com
contact@sunandmoonpublishing.com

ISBN 13: 978-0-9960295-2-0
ISBN 10: 0996029524
Printed in the United States of America

This diary is dedicated to my husband, George,
my children, Jamel, Randy and Anthony,
and my grandchildren, Jalen & Gianna.

It's also dedicated to all of my family and friends
who have helped me through this time in my life.
There are too many names and acts of kindness to mention,
but you know who you are, and the love you showed to me
and my family. Because of people like you,
I have been able to smile during this difficult time.
God sent me earthly Angels and I thank each of you
for allowing Him to use you. We will not forget any of you
and we appreciate all that you have done to make this journey
easier for us. Each of your contributions have helped
along the way in making this diary a reality and
I thank you from the bottom of my heart.

I can look back every day and see all the many blessings
God has given me---a supportive family, loving friends,
a supportive church family, Kingdom Touch Ministries
and prayers from so many. I am truly blessed.
Thank you Jesus for loving me and
I pray you can use my life for your glory...

Introduction

On May 10, 2011, my entire life changed......never to be the same. I heard these words spoken to me by my surgeon: "You have cancer." At that point, everything about my life changed. What will I do? Who will take care of my family? How long will I live? Two days later, I found out I have Stage IV Colon Cancer. What does that mean? How many stages are in cancer? When my nurse would not answer my questions, but told me to talk to my doctor, I knew I was in trouble; I knew it was not good. I felt numb inside, not sure what to say or do. It seemed like time stopped, and I did not want to feel or think about what I was about to go through. I learned that Stage IV is the last stage of the disease. But last stage doesn't mean this is the end. This journal records my thoughts, my concerns, my emotions, my testimony and my sanity while dealing with this dreadful disease. It helped me deal with it day by day. It includes memories that I will never forget, memories I want to share with others to help them during their journey, and words of inspiration that have helped me cope along the way. Proverbs 18:14 says, "The spirit of a man will sustain him in sickness." I know this to be true. Without my mind trusting totally in Jesus, I don't know where I would have been. I truly thank God for being my help and my strength. I choose to believe God's promises and stand on His Word. I felt God's presence in the hospital room that day and, though I was numb, I knew in my heart that "I shall not die but live and declare the works of the Lord." (Psalms 118:17)

God has been with me every minute of every hour, and I am so thankful to Him for His grace and mercy in my life. God allows us to go through challenges in our lives so that we can see ourselves and see if we are worthy of His blessings. I pray that I can pass the tests and deal with the hardships. I will continue to love God with all my heart, mind and soul, and to love His people to Him. I will continue to fight the good fight of faith until the very end.

May 10, 2011
Day One

It all started with gallstones that were causing me great pain. The doctors finally figured out why I had been having chest pains for the last two years. I had gone to the emergency room twice for pain in my chest, fearing I was having a heart attack. Thank God it wasn't my heart, but what the doctors found on this day was totally shocking. I would have never thought this would be happening to me. Why me, Lord? But, then, why not me? Who am I but a child of God trying each day to live a better and happier life? I can truly say that only by God's grace and mercy I was able to go through this storm. It is He who gave me the strength to go through each day. On this day, the doctor not only removed my gallbladder but also diagnosed me with Stage IV Colon Cancer!

What devastating news! No one wants to hear the words, "You have cancer." Those words were spoken to me by my doctor right after surgery on May 10, 2011, after he removed my gallbladder and received the biopsy results. I was in shock. I cried. When the doctor woke me up after surgery, he just came out with the news. Needless to say, I was already in pain, so when the doctor woke me up to share this news and I looked around at my husband and my three sons, I panicked and couldn't breathe. How can this be?

The doctor didn't know what he was talking about or, if he did, couldn't he have at least waited until tomorrow? I couldn't believe what I was hearing. What about my family? What would they do without me and who would take care of them? Lord, please help me. That's all I could say—"God, please help me." I knew my help comes only from the Lord, and He and only He could help me now.

My co-workers, Ms. Marsha and Mrs. Miranda, came to be with me and my family at the right time. They were there to comfort us, and I appreciated them so very much. As I looked at my sons, I could see that they were afraid. I couldn't even hug them and say that God will take care of me and things will be okay. I couldn't say anything. As I looked at my husband, he leaned over and kissed my forehead; though he was smiling, I knew he was hurting inside. He tried to be strong for me and his sons, but I could see the pain on his face. I could see he, too, was afraid. I am so very proud of him. He has been a wonderful protector, provider and friend. I am so glad God allowed me to marry such a wonderful man. I am so glad that we were able to go through the storms in our marriage and survive. He is my soul mate and I am grateful to God for him.

Those three simple words, "You have cancer," changed my life on that day. Those words can make your heart stop or make you feel paralyzed. The world around you seems to stop and you don't know what to do. I remembered a sermon I heard once on "What to do When You Don't Know What to do." The answer was simply to just look up to the hills where your help comes from. Well, I'm looking up right now and, with tears in my eyes, I am praying and waiting for a word from God. Lord, what must I do? I could only lie there on the hospital bed motionless, just looking up at the ceiling and waiting for an answer….. waiting for a word from the Lord. What do I do while I wait? All I know to do is to continue praying and hoping and believing that God is not finished with me yet. I know He's not….I'm praying He's not.

May 13, 2011

This was the day of my first surgery. After I was diagnosed two days ago, my doctors had to come up with a plan for me. They found tumors on my liver but knew that the cancer did not originate there. I had to have a colonoscopy yesterday, which confirmed that the cancer started in my colon. It's ironic that I had a colonoscopy just four weeks before and was told by my doctor that all was well and to come back in five years. Out of the 11 lymph nodes that were removed from my colon, 10 came back positive. My doctor came into my room after the colonoscopy to say that they wanted to do surgery right away to remove one-fourth of my colon. He also told me that the cancer had spread to my liver, which they call metastatic colorectal cancer. At this point, all I could do was to trust God. My life was in His hands. My doctor went on to discuss his plan for me, but before he walked out the door, I told him that though he has to report the facts to me according to medicine, I was going to believe the report of the Lord that says, "I shall not die but live and declare the works of the Lord." (Psalms 118:17) My doctor went to the door, turned around and looked at me, and said, "For some reason, I believe that your outcome will be good."

There was no one else I could trust or believe in but God and His Word. My life as I once knew it would never be the same. Everything around me became different. Now I have cancer. I know I must fight for my life. Later that day, I was introduced to my oncologist. He was highly recommended by my surgeon, and we were able to talk about the plans he had for me to start chemotherapy. I did not want to think or talk about that at all. I wanted to just wake up from this dream. It had to be a dream.

Again, I asked, "Why me, Lord?" The answer: "Why not you?"

May 24, 2011

Cancer has been a blessing in my life because it has made me realize how much I need the Lord in my life each and every day. It has made me see what is important in life: my relationship with God, my great family and my great friends. We really do take so much for granted in our lives. I had no idea how blessed my life is until now. It may seem crazy to say that cancer is a blessing, but it really brings you back to the things that are most important in life. Because we are such a busy people, we don't take the time to look into our lives to see how blessed we really are. Most of the time, we complain about what we don't have without thanking God for what we do have. What we need to do is spend more time with each other. It doesn't take much time for a phone call or a card in the mail or a short visit just to say, "I have been thinking about you and I love you." If I had only known then what I know now, I would have taken more time with my mother, who died in 2009, my children, my husband, my family and my friends. Life can be so short, and we have only one life to live. How so important it is to live life to the fullest! Now I realize how life can end at any moment; that alone will give you a completely different outlook on what's important in life. Every day is a gift. Every day is a blessing. Every day is a journey.

In my journey, I am able to see the Lord work through me. Because of His Word, I can now minister to others who are going through. I know, in spite of cancer, I have to move forward. There is life with cancer and after cancer. The Lord is truly directing my path. Someone called me to encourage me with words from Proverbs 18:14, "The spirit of a man will sustain him in sickness." How I deal with cancer will affect my outcome. I know that the Lord will heal me. His promises are sure. As I read back over my journals, I see where God was letting me know that I was going to "not die but live and declare the works of the Lord." (Psalms 118:17) He is allowing me to live, and I ask Him to help me be that "Daymaker" that I read about in a book that I received from Mrs. Faye at LeCreuset. I want to help encourage others to hold on to their faith, to our God, our Healer, our Redeemer. I have to trust God with everything inside me, knowing that He loves me so much.

Proverbs 3:5-6 says, "Trust in the Lord with all your heart, and lean not on your own understanding. In all your ways acknowledge Him, and He will direct your path." He surely has done this many times during this journey and is still faithfully doing it today.

I cannot end my writing today without giving honor to my family, friends, neighbors, church family at Kingdom Touch Ministries and my co-workers at LeCreuset of America. Food, flowers, books, calls, cards, gifts, money; you name it, it was there. Some even went grocery shopping for me and took me to my doctor's appointment. It's as if God sent angels to me. I can't believe how blessed I am to have such wonderful people in my life. My co-workers are no longer co-workers; they're friends. I did not know that such love existed among people, but it does, and we cannot forget that. Sometimes we don't believe that people love each other anymore, but I have found out that is a lie from the devil. There is love in this world and, as long as we believe in Jesus, we will continue to see God's magnificent love. It can't be hidden.

Life is no longer the same. I am living with cancer, a disease that has killed many. I must fight for my life and never give up. Though I have to fight as a good solider, I know that the battle has been won through Jesus Christ. The battle was won when He died on the cross for little me and you, and rose again on the third day. We serve a great God—what love! I have thought about what I would like people to remember about me and that is the legacy of love that can be passed on from generation to generation. Tina Turner asked a question in a song, "What's Love Got To Do With It?" Well, to answer her question, love has everything to do with it! So, each day, try to love more than you did the day before. If you are wondering if I got angry because I had cancer, my answer would be no. Why? Because if it hadn't been me, it might have been one of you. There are many horrible things that happen in life to good people, cancer being one of them, but one thing is for sure: there is nothing too hard for God. He is our healer. Jeremiah 30:17 says, "For I will restore you to health and heal your wounds, declares the Lord."

I don't know about you, but I believe Him!

May 29, 2011

So many thoughts are in my head. I am now home from the hospital with one-fourth of my colon gone. The doctors told us that the entire tumor in my colon was removed, but the tumors on my liver were too big to remove. I have to go through chemo so the tumors will shrink and be small enough to be removed. I am still in shock with all the things that are going on in my life. Here it was Sunday morning when I would normally be in church at Kingdom Touch Ministries. I'm in bed crying and thinking about the things that I cannot change. I'm praying for my brother-in-law and sister-in-law, who just lost their son, Brandon. Yes, in the midst of all of this, my husband lost a nephew. He was only 23 years old. There was no explanation about how he died. He just died. I can't imagine how they feel, and pray I never have to. I pray for his brother, Brenton. Lord, please be with him. I know in his mind he wants to know why his brother had to die. God, help him and the rest of us to understand.

We all know that one day we will die. Just help us to understand our time here on earth. Life can be so hard. How can I be lying here feeling sorry for myself when they have just lost their son? My husband and his sisters are on their way to Alabama to comfort their brother and family. God, please be with the family and give them the strength to get through this. I can't imagine how they are feeling right now.

God, help us to understand. How can I even think about what I'm going through right now? I do know that God promises not to bring more on us than we can bear. I know God will comfort the family. He promises to be there in the time of trouble. We will miss our good-looking nephew. We know he is in a much better place.

We love you, Brandon.

May 31, 2011

I'm thanking God for my husband and sons, who are staying close to me these days. I realize that I am not in this alone. Your entire family goes through all of this with you. My body is healing slowly. I can feel a difference in my body, but the good news is that I'm still here. I can't explain the loneliness I feel. Though I have my family and friends surrounding me, I still feel alone. My mind is thinking about so many things. I'm thinking about how life changes so fast. One minute you are here doing what you love; the next, you are told you have to have surgery, you need chemo, you can't go back to work, you need a second surgery, and so on and so on. In my mind, I don't know if I need to get things in order, like preparing my will. I probably need to do that anyway. Why do we wait until things happen to do what needs to be done? Yet, when I think about getting things in order, I feel as if I do not believe God's word, which says I will not die but live. What do you do? If I didn't trust God, I would be losing my mind right now. I don't want to show any doubt in my life. These are the things that you can't talk to anyone about because they will think you are giving up. That is not the case at all. Actually, I'm at a place I've never been before and just need some answers. Yes, I know to pray and ask God for direction, and I am doing that. My prayer is also that He will send an earthly angel to me to help me know where to go from here. I ask God to give me wisdom. I know He will.

June 7, 2011

It is Tuesday morning. Yes, Lord, I must confess I have been acting like a scared little girl. I don't know what to expect and where I'm going, but I do know that faith is believing without seeing. I know I have to trust you, God, with all that is inside of me. Just like your disciples asked you to increase their faith, I'm asking you, God, to increase mine. Without you, I will not make it. I need you so very much. This may seem crazy but, though my flesh wants to be scared, my spirit has peace, like it knows I'm going to be all right. It's a feeling of peace even when the storm is going on. That peace always allows me to know that everything is going to be all right. I know that peace can come only from you, Lord, and I thank you for it. God, you are awesome and you promise to make the crooked places straight. You have already gone before me, before my chemo treatments tomorrow, and I am so grateful. Where would I be without you? I'm so glad you also blessed me with a husband who has been a strong tower for me. Please bless George. Let everything he touches be blessed.

He is such a wonderful husband, father and friend. Bless him, Lord.

June 8, 2011
The Process

The process begins. This was the first day of chemo. I wanted to be afraid, but I actually felt the strength of God holding me up. I wanted to cry, but I couldn't. God wasnot only holding me up; He wouldn't let me cry either. I remember the nurse at the Cancer Center said, "If this were my first treatment, I would be so nervous." Well, what she didn't know was that God had His hands on me that day. I was leaning on Him. I was just trusting God for the outcome. It was as if I was numb. I was walking around and had no emotions. Yes, God was holding me up. He knew I couldn't handle all of this on my own. I would have to go to Charleston Cancer Center every other week until I received 12 rounds of chemotherapy. My treatments would be on Wednesday through Friday every other week. I didn't want to think about it. I had no idea how I would get through this. Not on my own anyway. I knew God would be there to help me, but I still wondered what was going to happen and whether I could really make it through this ordeal. My doctor was a godsend. He reminded me that healing belongs to God and he was there just to do his part. That gave me so much hope.

As the nurse took me to his office to do the blood work, reality set in. This was really happening. My surgeon had implanted a port in my chest a week before, and now I was about to have my first chemo treatment. The nurse tried to make the needle-stick through the port pleasant. Yes, it hurt. I was still sore from the port being implanted just a week ago. After reading my blood work, the nurse took me to a room they call the Cancer Suite. I looked around and saw that cancer does not discriminate. There were black, white, old, and young people there. What a sight to see, and I was among them. I took the window seat and was able to look at the lake outside. That was refreshing. The nurse came and hooked me up to the nausea medicine first. This process took around 30 minutes. Then she replaced that bag with my first chemo treatment. This process lasted two and a half hours.

They gave everyone a blanket and pillow so you can rest as the chemo goes into your system, but I couldn't fall asleep. How can you? My sons brought me to my first treatment, but they did not want to stay there to watch this being done, so they went to the mall. I was glad they did. I hated seeing the sadness in their faces. I knew they hated the fact that I had to go through all this. As I was sitting there waiting until the treatment ended, I started texting my friends and family to let them know that I was doing well. If only they could see how God was holding me up. I knew it was Him. I still couldn't cry. My husband texted me many times to check on me. I knew he was concerned. All I could say is, "I am so very glad that God is my strength."

After the first chemo treatment was over, the nurse hooked me up for my second treatment, which I was able to take home with me by connecting it to a pump for 46 hours. Yes, I had to wear a bag and a pump—my new "buddy"—for two days. What an experience that was and is. I was to be connected to this treatment from Wednesday until Friday. I couldn't sleep the first night I received it. I thought I would disconnect it or something. I sat and watched television most of the night. The steroids in the medicine made me hyper most of the night. I was also nauseous from the chemo treatment. I woke up at 3:30 a.m. to vomit. This, too, was awful, but my husband was right there by my side. I began to cry. Yes, now I was able to cry. I felt so bad.

The next day I felt so tired. The fatigue was terrible and I had a fever. I wasn't just tired; it was worse than that. I read the information about side effects, which explained the feeling as fatigue, and that is just what I felt. I felt so tired and wanted to just stay in bed. There was also the nausea and the sick feeling I felt in my chest. By that night, I could feel the chemo in my bones, my flesh. I could even smell it. I didn't want to eat but made myself do it because I wanted to survive. I finally took medication for my nausea. Unfortunately, the pill would not stay down so I cried myself to sleep yet again. I can't really explain how I felt. I just knew that I would not wish this on my worst enemy. The other side effect was diarrhea. That meant I woke up every hour on the hour to use the bathroom.

When my husband left for work, I laid in bed and cried and cried. I needed to. I have heard that crying is good for the soul. Well, this day I was going to find out if it is true. I felt absolutely terrible. There are no words to explain it. You would have to walk in my shoes to understand how I felt that day. I prayed and prayed for God to help me through those side effects. I prayed and prayed that God would heal me. I knew He would, but I also knew that I had to go through the process. This was my process and no matter how frustrated I was, I had to go through it. I had to recognize what the Lord was doing. I had to understand what He was doing in my life. Yes, I did ask God why, and I am still waiting for the answer. I know He will answer me, but in the meantime, I have to go through this process. I only ask God to strengthen me to go through. I know He will. He promised never to leave me or forsake me.

Everything you've heard about chemo is true. I wondered how people tolerated it, but now I understand that you will do what it takes to live. The chemo gave us hope, and I knew that with help from Jesus Christ, I would be able to tolerate it because I wanted to live. Though the chemo made me sick, caused me to be so fatigued I didn't want to walk, and killed my appetite, I just kept on going. When anyone asked how I was doing, I just smiled and said I am doing fine because I knew I would be.

June 10, 2011

I woke up Friday morning very tired. I couldn't keep my eyes open on the way to the Cancer Center. My sisters took me to Summerville so they could remove my chemo pump, which had been there since Wednesday. My sisters looked at my face that day and I could see the concern on their faces. I'm blessed to have so much support around me. I was so glad to be taking the pump off. My first treatment was not easy but, by the grace of God, I got through it. I remember calling on Him each time I felt sick or felt pain, and He always helped me. I prayed, "Lord, strengthen me to endure as a good soldier." I read Psalms 33:20, which says, "My soul waits on you, Lord." God is my help and my shield. Lord, where would I be without you?

When I think back on my life, I remember loving God's word so much that when I just thought about it, I got excited. I remember reading His Word and going to bed preaching to myself. I shared the Word of God with whoever would listen to me. I also remember getting so busy that I stopped reading like I used to. Wow, how can we allow so many distractions to come in our lives and take the one thing that is important? I am so glad God is a forgiving God. I'm so glad that He is not like man. Now I have time to read and study God's Word again. I have time to listen to Him and, right now, I need a word. I know it's the Word of God that's going to keep me through these treatments. I completed Round1, and I made it through. Lord, help me to go to each of my treatments with a smile on my face. Though I have to go through them, I know that this, too, shall pass.

June 14, 2011

It is 5:33 p.m. God, you are so good! I was able to drive to Hampton to pick up my medicine today. It was good to get out. We take so much for granted. I never thought I would be this happy just to drive my truck again. I can't explain the excitement I felt. It may sound crazy but it doesn't feel that way. I am grateful to be able to drive myself again. Another blessing happened today as well. Johnson C. Smith University called to say that they awarded Anthony a small Pell grant for this semester. Now that was good news. Any amount helps. I just want Anthony to have all he needs to get his degree. We are so proud of Anthony.

Then my son, Randy, blessed me by taking "Thinking of You" cards to my job for the employees to write a note to me in them. Wasn't that a blessing! Randy can be so thoughtful. I still can't believe he did that. He came home and brought me a bunch of cards with words of encouragement in them, all signed by my former co- workers. I cried, as always. I asked him what made him do that and he said he wanted to make me smile. Well, it worked because I'm still smiling. That blessed my soul. I called Ms. Marsha, and she said everyone was impressed by what Randy did.

I feel mighty blessed today. That was so touching. Can you imagine the happiness I felt to have so many people who love me? What do I have to complain about? I pray that my co-workers felt the love of God by Randy's actions. I know I did. Sometimes our children don't show their love for us. I think they take us for granted.

Actually, I know they do, just like I did with my parents. Thank God, I grew up and understood the sacrifices my mom made just for me. I knew she loved me so much. I'm so glad I felt her love. And this day, I felt Randy's love for me. Even though I know he loves me, it's good sometimes to see it. Yes, today was a great day and, Lord, I am truly grateful.

I received other calls today as well. My sister-in-law, Jackie, called with encouraging words and a promise to send me the Bible study they were teaching at her church. Dr. Shealy returned my call to talk to me about my diabetes medicine. I have to adjust it because of the chemo, but things will be okay. Pastor Lewis called to encourage me, and I thank God for it. Today, God, I felt your love and your compassion, and I thank you for placing so many great people in my life.

June 15, 2011

My soul does magnify the Lord. My soul waits for you, Lord. You are my help and my shield. Lord, where would I be without you? I remember getting revelation from God's Word. I remember when I couldn't wait until I could share God's Word with someone. I remember being so excited that I would look at my desk at work and I could see the Bible sitting there. I could actually see the page numbers. That may seem crazy, but I remember those things.

I'm sitting here now wondering where the excitement went. What happened in life to take that excitement away? When and where did I lose the joy of my salvation? Lord, please show me what happened in life that made me forget about you. What is so important in life that we place it before God? I have thought about it over and over again. Then something clicked in my head. I remembered being so busy with work, church, family, and other things, and forgetting about God. I didn't prioritize my life. I stopped doing the important things, like spending time with God. I thought being busy was my purpose in life. If I wasn't busy, I felt like I wasn't doing anything. I had to be at all the right places, or so I thought. Don't get me wrong. Serving others is important. But you have to have balance. Spending time with God every day is so very important. Somehow I lost my way. I listened to others, did as they said I should do, and didn't listen to the voice of God.

Now that I am alone and still, I can, once again, hear from Him. Why didn't I see that before? I never listened and asked God what He wanted me to do. Lord, what is Your Will for my life? What do you want me to do? I'm asking God today to make me all over again, to take me to the potter's wheel and make me into the vessel He wants me to be, a vessel that is pleasing to His sight. Teach me; show me what you would have me do. Then help me to be a blessing to others. I thank you Lord for my lesson today.

June 23, 2011
This was the day after my treatment...

The day after treatment is much better than the day of treatment. I had a fever last night of 100.8 degrees. My legs were aching and my body felt so tired. I have never been so tired and achy in my life. As always, I called upon the Lord and He answered me. I am so glad I know the Lord. I don't know what I would do without Him. These treatments are so hard but I know I have to continue the process. God will bring me through each one of them. I'm depending on Him. My confidence is in Him. Lord, again help me......

June 29, 2011

Lord, here I am to worship you. I love you and want to please you. I have gone through another round of chemo. Now I am having fever at night and my legs are aching. My body feels so tired, but I again called upon the Lord and, again, He answered me. I am so glad I know the Lord and He is my savior. During all of this, we received news that Aunt Patsy died Saturday morning at 1:40 a.m. It seems unreal. I talked to her only a week ago. Though she sounded weak, she talked and knew who I was. I'm sitting here today thinking about my own life. How can I ever feel sorry for myself? I'm still here among the living. What a wonderful thing, to be here. I could be dead. I know it's you, Lord, allowing me to live. I pray for my aunt's son and family. May she rest in perfect peace. The Word of God tells us to rejoice when one dies. I rejoiced for Aunt Patsy. I rejoiced with her family.

July 5, 2011

God, how awesome is your name in Heaven and on Earth. Here I am again wondering about life. I had a dream last night and am wondering what it meant. As I think about this dream, I see now that I will pass this test that I'm going through. Thank you, Lord, for allowing me to see in this dream your grace and mercy, and how you always give us another chance to pass the test. My dream began in a classroom setting. I could see the desks, the students, and the teacher, though I couldn't see their faces. The teacher had given us a test, and as I looked at it, I knew I would fail it because I hadn't studied. I glanced over the test and saw that the questions were true or false. I read some of the questions and knew the answers to some of them, but not enough to pass the test. It appeared that only one person, a young lady in the class, finished the test; I could see her handing the test to the teacher. As she walked back to her desk, she looked back and smiled. I looked around and it appeared that no one else had studied for the test either. The teacher stood up and said she was giving us another chance to take the test the next day. I remember thinking that this time I would study and pass it. I knew I could do it, especially since the teacher had shown us mercy and was giving us another chance. I looked at the test again and I saw one particular question that stood out to me. There were two pairs of shorts designed one way and two more pairs designed another way. I put two of the same pair to my left and the other design to my right. As I looked at them, I could see that there was a pattern being made. Though the shorts were different designs, I knew somehow they were coming together to make one design. I thought about the pattern and wanted to rush home to study more about it and to study for the test so I could pass it the next day.

This was a dream, but I remembered it clearly. I could see the teacher, and the other students looking down at their tests, and none of us but the one young lady seemed to know the answers. What was so great about it was that the teacher knew we didn't know the answers and was giving us another chance to study for it. What a dream! Thank God for giving me another chance to pass my test. I now know that, by the grace and mercy of God, I will pass the test that I'm going through right now. I thank the Lord, for confirming it for me.

July 12, 2011

Today I had a meeting with my bosses at LeCreuset of America. I knew that this meeting would be hard for them just as it would be hard for me. No matter what we go through, life goes on. It doesn't stop because of our storms. The good news is that a storm never lasts forever. If you have ever watched the clouds during a storm, you've noticed that they keep moving rapidly. The clouds never seem to stop in one area; they keep moving, keep going to another place. I'm so grateful that the storm doesn't last forever. That's why we have to keep moving. We have to hold on to our faith until the storm passes by, knowing that it will be over soon. I found this to be true on this day of July. Life goes on, and we have to keep going in spite of the changes we have to make.

On this day, my bosses informed me that they had to fill my position at work; they could no longer hold it open for me. I could see that they prepared themselves to tell me. I could tell that they were trying to be strong. You could look in their faces and see that they, too, were trying not to cry. I wanted to scream. I wanted to ask God why. I wanted to know why my life had to change so much. Everything was different. When I left my job on Tuesday, May 10, 2011, for gallbladder surgery, I never dreamed that I would not come back to it. I loved my job so very much. God, it was you who blessed me with it. The Lord gives and He takes away. Yes, I feel really hurt that I'm no longer there. I feel hurt knowing that all I worked hard for is gone, but I know God will take care of me and my family.

My position at LeCreuset is gone but God's promises are true, and His Word says in Isaiah 61:7, "Instead of your shame you shall have double honor, and instead of confusion they shall rejoice in their portion. Therefore in their Lord they shall possess double; everlasting joy shall be theirs. For the Lord loves justice." This Word lets me know that there is something better that God has for me, and everything will be all right. I will receive double blessings for my trouble. I took the news and smiled, but I was really hurting inside. All I wanted to do was just get in my car so I could cry it out. I did that. I cried, and cried, and cried. I had to. I found out that crying really helps to remove the pain and hurt and disappointment. It's not a sign of weakness. It just proves that you are human and you have a heart that loves and cares. I thank God for the tears. God says he will wipe the tears from our eyes. God, please wipe mine.

July 13, 2011

I was sad because of my meeting yesterday. I loved my job at LeCreuset. You don't realize how blessed you are until you lose something. That's how I felt. I felt that I have lost everything I have worked so hard for. My first job at LeCreuset was Retail Accountant for the stores. God blessed me with a new position after a few years at the company. I became LeCreuset Payroll Accountant. I felt hurt knowing that all my hard work is now gone. I do understand the company's position. No, I'm not blaming anyone. I know I can't go back to work right now, but that doesn't mean I don't feel the hurt and pain of losing something I loved. Mrs. Faye took George and me to dinner. She encouraged me and gave me hope that something much better will come my way. I am so thankful for caring co-workers who care about me and my family. Elaine and Archie were great bosses. I know that the meeting yesterday was as hard for them as it was for me. As I think about the things that have happened to me since May 10, 2011, I know that if it were not for the Lord keeping my mind sound, I could have lost it. God is my strength.

July 19, 2011

Thursday, I took off alone and drove myself to Beaufort I really needed to get out of the house and my surroundings so I could forget about all that had happened and focus on other things. I had a great day. I felt stronger in my body and was so grateful. Last night we went to Bible study at Pastor Eady's church in Varnville. It was a blessing, as always. Randy and Anthony were obedient and came with us. Pastor Eady prayed for all of us. We all needed it. I know my sons are worried about me. I wish Jamel had been there with us, but I know prayer can reach him in Augusta.

What is so amazing about this day is that it is our 30th wedding anniversary. I am so glad God gave us the wisdom and strength to fight for our marriage and our family. It was not easy, but we have come a long way. I wish we could have gone on a much needed trip for our anniversary, but maybe next time. I am so grateful for God's grace and mercy on our marriage. I can't believe I am still married to George after 30 years. That's a long time. The good news is that our marriage has gotten so much better as we have grown older and received Christ in our lives. We really can't do anything without Him. God taught us how to love Him and each other. We have fallen back in love with each other, and it is so good. That may not make sense to others, but, for George and me, we know that love can become stale and you have to keep falling in love. It's a beautiful thing, love is.

July 25, 2011

Today I am having the Monday morning blues. Lord, I don't know what you are doing in my life, but I just want to thank you. No, this is not what I wanted to be writing. I wanted to complain and tell you how much I'm hurting inside, but, for some reason, all I can say today is thank you. Forgive me, Lord, for all the doubts and fears that come my way, and help me to continue to trust you for my healing. The enemy is always there with all of his lies, but I rebuke them in Jesus' name. I trust you with my life. I feel totally stripped down to nothing. All of my pride is gone and all that I thought I had going for me is now gone. My total dependence is on you. Jesus, let Your Will be done in my life. I am so glad that, in spite of the Monday morning blues, I can bless the Lord anyway!

July 31, 2011

The men at KTM were celebrating their second Men's Conference. My husband went to the conference every night and I am so very proud of him. It took great sacrifice to work in the heat all day and then go to church every night. He even attended the Saturday workshops. I can see George growing in the Lord. Please, God, bless him with all the desires of his heart. You blessed me with a wonderful husband and I thank you for helping me to not give up on our marriage when things were bad. Co-pastor Crystal preached a sermon called, "Everything Dead Doesn't Need to be Buried." I'm glad we didn't bury our marriage because it was dead at one time. God knew we would make it. God knew we would persevere. Thanks, Lord, for helping us endure as good soldiers.

August 4, 2011

This was the day after my fifth treatment, though the pump won't be removed until tomorrow. I had a fever again but, thank God, it was only for a few hours this time. I felt really bad earlier and endured more pains in my legs; all I could do was cry out to the Lord. I am so grateful to know God hears my cry. Who wouldn't serve a God like that! One that we can call and He will answer. Thank you, Lord. I am learning how to eat before and after my treatments. I found out that eating a good breakfast before going to treatment was my best option because after treatment I have no appetite. I'm glad a friend came by my home to share her testimony with me and to give me some very helpful advice. She told me to make sure to eat a good breakfast and I have found that to be true. After my treatments, all I want to do is go to bed even if I can't sleep. I just lie there and rest and watch television. That's all the energy I have after treatments. I am so glad that I have treatments every other week instead of every week. I know things could be worse. After about five days, my appetite usually comes back and I can eat again, even if only to get my body ready for the next treatment. This is working for me so far and I know it will continue to work. Thanks, God, for friends who continue to encourage me. I hate every moment of my treatments, but when I think about my life, my family, and my friends, I know I have so much to live for.

August 12, 2011

Lord, you are so awesome. I thank you for restoring my health and healing my wounds as you said you would in Jeremiah 30:17. I thank you for allowing me to "not die but live and declare the works of the Lord." (Proverbs 118:17). This week, KTM had its Vacation Bible School and it was very successful. You have given that ministry a spirit of excellence, and it shows in all that they do. I really enjoyed teaching the adult class. The Word of God truly blessed me and I hope it blessed others.

This week I had a doctor's appointment in Walterboro. My doctor there told me I have lots of hope, but it's not just hope I have—my faith also keeps me. Yes, the hope is much needed and we must keep hope alive, but, without faith, we cannot please God. My faith is in the promises of God. I have to believe His Word. I have learned that when you get to the point in life when all you have is God, then you will find out that He is all you need. He is the one who brings everything else in your life together for your good. Who else can do that?

August 17, 2011

I had my sixth treatment this day and guess what? I have the victory! This is the first time I did not get nauseous or have the sick feeling in my chest. Best of all, I had no fever! God is so good. I am a little tired, but I can handle that just by resting. I am celebrating today because my God is awesome. Today the enemy has lost because greater is He on the inside of me than he that is in the world. I am so excited. I will be having a CAT scan Monday. I am claiming that cancer is gone from my liver and the rest of my body, in Jesus' name. I know God is able to do it. In the meantime, I will continue to wait on my God.

August 21, 2011

Sunday morning and feeling blue, basically because I can't do the things I used to do or go the places I used to go. Lord, help me be content in the state I'm in. Just a few days ago I was singing the victory song. Now it feels like I am losing, but I know that's a lie from the enemy. Victory is mine, says the Lord. I know God is able to do just what He says He will do. Help me to walk through the process. Help me to not feel sorry for myself, but see that the glory of God will be manifested in my life. Psalms 19:14 says "Let the words of my mouth and the meditation of my heart be acceptable in your sight, O Lord, my strength and my redeemer." Change my words to your words; change my desires to your desires, dear Lord. I'm sad because I watched my family going in and out of the house and I'm usually there with them. Now, all I can do is watch them. I never knew the emotions you have to go through during sickness. I truly will be more compassionate to others who are going through any sickness. It's more than just the physical side of this; it's also the spiritual and mental emotions you have to deal with. Teach me, Lord, so I can help others to go through.

August 24, 2011

I was listening to Beth Moore this morning teaching about Joseph being in the pit. I understood just what she was talking about, how man can place you in the pit. I could see myself once being in the pit and allowing man to bring me out only to place me in bondage. Man will make you feel like you owe him something when he helps lead you to Christ, not realizing that it's God who is doing it the whole time. The Bible says one plant, one water, but it's God who gives the increase. God is the one who can bring us out of the pit, and He uses people to do it. Why, then, do we allow people to put us into bondage? It's not people who can bring you out of the pit in the first place, but God, using them as His vessel. I am asking God to bring me out of my pit of doubts, fears and insecurities, and show me how to walk into my purpose. Show me how to love your people, God, and to help them out of their pit and out of bondage. Don't allow me to be prideful and think it's me and not God that's in me doing the work.

Never allow me to place others into bondage. God, please show me the way.

1 Corinthians 3:5-7 (NKJV)

"Who then is Paul, and who is Apollos, but ministers through whom you believed, as the Lord gave to each one? I planted, Apollos watered, but God gave the increase. So then neither he who plants is anything, nor he who waters, but God who gives the increase."

September 1, 2011

I am forever grateful for your tender mercies and your amazing Grace. Where would I be without you? In spite of how things look I know that you will never leave me nor forsake me. I am going through my 7th treatment. I only have five more treatments to go! I know the Lord is taking me through every treatment. Thank you for being my strength.

Today has been a great day. Ms. Marsha came to see me and brought me lunch from "Paula's." It was good and fresh as always. I miss eating lunch there. Ms. Marsha is a true friend and I thank God for her. I hope one day I can be a blessing to her. On tomorrow, Jamel and Annette Mole will be taking me to Charleston to remove my pump. I am so thankful for everyone's help. We could not do this without our family and friends. God you have supplied us with all of our needs and we thank you.

September 3, 2011

Today, George, Jamel and Randy went to Charlotte for Anthony's football game. I had a chemo treatment this week so I was weak and nauseous and unable to go. I was happy that George and the boys went to support Anthony. After they walked out of the house and got into the truck, tears fell from my eyes. I was trying to be strong for George, but it hurt me so much to be left behind. Again, I felt the loneliness. This was the first time my family went to Anthony's game without me. My life has changed so much. There was a time when the truck didn't move without me being in it; now I can't go to my son's football game. Life goes on, and I don't want my family to stop living and supporting each other because of me. Every other weekend I'm at home too tired and nauseous to do anything. But I know things could be a lot worse. Lord, I'm not complaining but, again, asking you for your comfort and strength. I read today in 2 Timothy what Paul said about God preserving him. That's exactly how I feel today, that Jesus has preserved me. He has kept me. I have been through so much and I know if it had not been for the Lord, where would I be? Help me endure like a good soldier.

What's amazing is God is always on time. Right after my family left, my boss, Elaine, came over and brought me lots of food. She had stuffed bell peppers, field peas, rice, chicken pot pie, catfish stew and a blueberry pound cake. Wow, it's so good to know that others love you. Then, another car came and my sisters, Linda and Gloria, stopped by to see me. Talk about God being on time! He didn't want me to be lonely, so He sent his earthly angels to be with me until my family came back home. God is so good to us. He knows what we need before we do. I have to laugh because God is so amazing. He sends people at the right moment.

September 8, 2011

Today I decided to write a "bucket list," my list of dreams. Some of them may not make sense to others but they do to me. I'm always thinking about other people. What are my dreams and things I would like to do? Well, here are some of them. I have plenty more but want to list just a few:

- To become a woman of God who helps others see how great and mighty God is.
- To become a servant of God; to serve others and teach others how to serve.
- To make a difference in the lives of others so they can make a difference in more lives. Pass it on.
- To make a difference in my children's and grandchildren's lives; for them to see God in me and know that He is real so they, too, will want to live for Him. To be an example.
- To go to the Holy Land Experience in Orlando, Florida.
- To take my grandson, Jalen, and my entire family to Carowinds and not have to worry about finances. I want to enjoy them and want them to enjoy me.
- To be able to speak to women across the USA and the world about Jesus; to be able to touch their hearts with the Word of God. No one will go home the same way they came.
- To travel and visit with family and friends; go to the beach; see beautiful places and experience different things.
- To do talk radio. Speak the Word of God on radio. To speak words of encouragement to others.
- To see my friends, Annette and Gary, get remarried.

September 13, 2011

Here I am to worship. That's what I feel like doing today. I received my first disability check this week. To some people, that may not mean a thing, but, to me, it means survival. This check came at the right time. My husband is a wonderful provider, but I know he needs help. We need help to pay our bills, which include many medical bills. All I could say was, "Thank you, God." I paid as many bills with the check as I could. I used it all. I wanted to take as much pressure off my husband as I could. Not only did I get my disability check, I also received the decision from SSDI that I was approved. I have to put all my trust in God. I have to believe that God will supply all my needs. God is able. That is the song I kept hearing and playing before I went into the hospital. Little did I know that the song was for me. The song ministered to my heart and I kept playing it over and over again. Now I know that God is able. He is able to do just what He said He would do. God has shown that to me every day of my life. He promised to never leave me or forsake me, and I believe Him.

September 22, 2011
Packing Day

I will call this day the "Packing Day." It's the day that I was not looking forward to, the day I had to clean out my office at LeCreuset. I thought I would be strong enough to handle it, but I found out I was wrong. I know I shouldn't look at it as a bad day, but as a day of thanksgiving. Why? Because I know it was the Lord who gave me this job, and now He will be opening up new opportunities for me. I heard the knocking at the door in a dream the night before. The sound was so real that I got out of bed to look out the window because I thought someone really was knocking at the door. Now I know that the knocking was to let me know that I will have greater opportunities knocking at my door when the Lord releases me to go back to work, either for the company or for Him. God, just help me to be patient. This is not easy at all.

I cried while I was packing my personal things in boxes. I still sometimes can't believe all of this is happening to me. What can I say? The Lord gives and the Lord takes away......glory be to God. Yes, God, I do want to ask you why and I will wait for the answer. I know now that it's okay to question God. Who else can I ask that has the answer? No man can answer our questions. No one has the answers but God....so, God, please answer me why. God, please continue to give me peace with all that is happening in my life. I must trust God no matter what I am going through.

It was God who provided me with the job, along with the wisdom to do it. I remember my first few weeks doing payroll. I was so very scared that I would not be able to perform my duties. It was so overwhelming at the time, but I kept praying that God would give me the knowledge to do it. The accounting part of the job looked like Greek. I had no idea what I was doing, but one day, the pieces of the puzzle came together for me. God answered my prayers. As weeks went by, it became easier. I knew if it was Him who gave me the job, then He had to give me the knowledge to perform it. God will enable you to do just what He wants you to do. He doesn't give you a task and not give you the knowledge to complete it. Even though there were times that I fussed about deadlines and the amount of work I had, I really did love my job and the people I worked with.

Yes, my job in payroll/accounting had come a long way, and now I had to give it all up. I know it will be for something much better. God never decreases in His giving; He always increases. I can't wait until He gives me double for my trouble. I know you will do it, Lord. Help me to be patient to receive it. I really didn't want to take any of that stuff home. That stuff belongs in my office. My husband stopped me as I was leaving the job and wanted to know why the sad face. It's not because I don't trust what God is doing, but because this is part of the process and it hurts going through it. Well, I know God has a bigger and better plan for my life, and I can't wait until He leads me there. I just ask God to strengthen my heart, mind and soul until that day comes. I need you, Lord, to do this. I can't do it without you. As the song says, "He has His hands on me."

September 29, 2011

This was the day after my ninth chemo treatment at the Cancer Center and my second chemo treatment at the hospital. I am now taking a third chemo along with what I was taking at the Cancer Center. My insurance will not pay for this chemo unless it is administered at the hospital, so I arrive at the Cancer Center for my first treatment of the third type. After two and a half hours, I go to the hospital for more hours, only to turn around and go back to the Cancer Center to receive my third treatment in the pump to take home for 46 hours. For some reason, I had to wait an extremely long time for my treatment at the hospital, but what else could I do but wait? My friend, Angie, took me to this treatment, and she was a true blessing from God. She had so much patience and compassion. Every one of my friends or family who takes me to my treatments has been a blessing to me. It's so many people that I can't even name them all.

The hospital's cancer center is smaller, but there were times when a woman came around and song to the patients. She had a very good voice. I asked her profession and she said that she was a music therapist. I never heard of that before, but what a blessing to have a gift like that and to be able to use it to help people. She was able to sing any song we named. What a rewarding career that would be. The nurses at the hospital were especially nice. They actually feed you during your treatments, but who can eat? Most of the time, I try to go to sleep so when I wake up it will be time to go back to the Cancer Center.

I never imagined what others go through to survive. We never pay attention to what others are going through until we have to go through. This will definitely make me more aware of other people's problems and the things they are going through. Yes, I will have more compassion towards others and pray more and more for them. My life is different, but I am seeing now that the differences are making me a better person.

October 5, 2011

God, you are awesome no matter what life looks like. Yes, it seems as if so much is happening, not just in my life, but in the lives of others as well. All of us have this question in the back of our minds: "Why do bad things happen to good people?" None of us have the answer, but we know that God is the answer and He knows the plans He has for each of us. Two days ago my first cousin died from a blood clot. Why, Lord? She was only 41 years old. I can't imagine how her parents and sibling feel right now. All I know is that they need your strength. God, please comfort them all. The family needs you so much. Please give them understanding of Your Word. We know that Your Will is to give us life, and life more abundantly. We need you, Lord, for comfort at this time of so much pain. In the midst of so many deaths, you still allow me to live, and I thank you. I know you have work for me to do, so please continue to heal my body so that I can do Your Will. When I heard about my cousin's death, I also heard of another great woman of God who was diagnosed with cancer. Please, God, heal her. Let her live her life to the fullest. Give her peace in the midst of her sickness. Help her trust you the more. Comfort her family.

October 11, 2011

Today is my 47th birthday. I am so excited because I lived to see another birthday! What a great God we serve. I love you, Lord, for your faithfulness. You have been so very good to me. No matter what it looks like or how I may feel, I know that you have healed and restored my body. I will not doubt the work you have done in my body for your glory. God, I will praise you with everything inside of me. I wanted to get out of bed and get dressed today to celebrate my life. I wanted to let you know how much I love you and thank you for the things you have done. Thanks for letting me "not die but live and declare the works of the Lord." (Psalms 118:17)

October 14, 2011

Today I completed my 10th round of treatment. My pump came off, and I was so glad. I am tired and nauseous, but God is strengthening me through each treatment. What's amazing is that my white blood counts have never gone under 4.0. I get a copy of my blood work at each treatment, and every time I ask my doctor about my blood work, he says, "Amazing." As I look at the sheet now, there is no explanation but God. He is keeping my blood regulated. I have not had any shot or medicine to boost my white blood cells. The Lord is so faithful. When we call, He promises to answer us. Words can't express how I feel right now. I know that God is able to bring us through every trial, every situation, every problem, and every test. He wants us to have the victory. He wants us to be winners, so that's why He goes before us to make every crooked place straight. Things can be scary at times, but if we continue to trust God with our health, with our life, with our finances, He promises to work them out. What to do when you don't know what to do is, simply, trust God. You must believe His Word and lean on Him. Your faith has to be strong and in Him. You must know that He loves you and wants the best for you.

Thank you, Lord.

Prov 3: 5-6; 1 Chron 28:9-10 (be strong...); Jer 10:23
Ps 37: 3-6, 23-24; Prov 24:16
Is 58:14a
Ps 55:22
Prov 34:19
Job 5: 18-19
Micah 7:8

October 24, 2011

There are days when you feel so happy, days when you feel you have no problems in your life at all. This day is one of those days for me. I feel completely healed. I don't know why I feel that way, but I do. It's a great feeling.

I was able to eat today. In fact, I had been eating all day long. As I was eating earlier, I laughed because it was a day that I could eat and not feel nauseous. I was eating everything in sight. I am forever grateful, Lord. It's crazy how we take so much for granted. We get up each morning without taking the time to thank God for the little things in life, such as being able to eat a simple meal. Today, Lord, I thank you for helping me see that each day is truly a gift. Thanks for reminding me of my gifts. I feel this way each week before my next treatment. God is always preparing me for the next treatment by reminding me of His goodness.

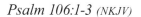

Psalm 106:1-3 (NKJV)

"Praise the Lord! Oh, give thanks to the Lord, for He is good! For His mercy endures forever. Who can utter the mighty acts of the Lord? Who can declare all His praise? Blessed are those who keep justice, and he who does righteousness at all times!"

October 26, 2011

Wow! This is my 11th treatment—just one more to go. I am so happy to know that it's almost over. I'm not excited about taking this treatment right now, but about knowing that the next time I come we will be celebrating my completion of 12 rounds of chemo. All I can think about is the next time. I know I have to get through this treatment first, but just knowing that I will have only one more helps me to forget about the chemo going through my veins. Nothing has changed about the treatments. I go to the Cancer Center for two and a half hours, then around the corner to the hospital for the other treatment. Then I come back to be hooked up to my third treatment, which I take home with me. I'm so glad the treatment at the hospital is only one hour now. I'm enjoying the entertainment they have for the patients. The music therapy is great, and once they even brought around a huge dog to pet. Needless to say, I was afraid of him because he was so big, but he did take my mind off the treatment for a moment. As always, I take a nap so the time goes by faster. I keep reminding myself there is only one more treatment to go.

I am so grateful for God's promise that says He will never leave us or forsake us. I am so glad to know that God is with me through every treatment, every surgery, every needle-stick, every CAT scan. I know that now I will have more compassion for those who are going through cancer. I never knew how hard this journey is until now. I guess those who say, "Unless you walk in my shoes, you will never know what I have gone through" are right. That saying is true because I never would have guessed how awful this journey could be. I always wondered if chemo was as bad as others said it was and, if it was, why in the world people took it. Well, now I can answer all of these questions. Yes, chemo is bad, but you take it because you choose to live and will do whatever it takes to keep living. Yes, chemo makes you sick. It makes you tired. It makes you hurt all over, especially your legs. Yes, it makes you nauseated each and every day, but when you think about the positive side, which is the fact that it is helping you to live, you learn to tolerate it. Yes, that's all you are doing, tolerating it. You just keep going and going because you have hope that each chemo treatment is giving you more years to live. You know that your healing comes from God, but if He chooses to heal you through chemo, then you go through it. I have learned to accept those things I cannot change.

I don't know why God is allowing me to go through this journey with the chemo. I know that, if He wants, I can be healed right now. If not, I am asking Him for the strength to get through each and every treatment I have to take. Thanks, God.

Ps 100: 1-5 Enter unto His Gates . . .

Psalm 31:1-2 (NKJV)

"In You, O Lord, I put my trust; Let me never be ashamed; Deliver me in Your righteousness. Bow down Your ear to me, Deliver me speedily; Be my rock of refuge, a fortress of defense to save me. For You are my rock and my fortress; Therefore, for Your name's sake, Lead me and guide me."

November 3, 2011

This is what the Lord spoke to me this morning as I was reading and worshipping Him. I am to remember this day when the Lord has spoken in my spirit about 2012, which is to be the year that He will bless me beyond measure. As I was lying down and watching TBN this morning, a thought came to me about the number 2012. This number was my extension at work and it is the number for me to remember God's grace and mercy. I don't know and understand all God is saying to me this morning, but I know He will give me revelation. The words from Him were, "You may have lost your job and all that goes with it, but you will gain so much more." I will begin to see the blessings even more in 2012. God's grace and mercy will take me to that place of victory and mighty blessings. Let every blessing for me also become a blessing to someone else. Amen.

November 6, 2011

God is so very good. This Sunday, 17 people at Kingdom Touch Ministries were ordained. Even though some of us were ordained at other ministries, we officially received our license from KTM. That was amazing because this was my husband's first ordination service. He officially was licensed as a minister. I am so very proud of him. My prayer for him is that God blesses him with His wisdom, knowledge and understanding. Give him the courage and confidence to do the works of the Lord. I pray that my husband has a mountaintop experience, as Moses did, and God allows him to see His glory. Not just George, but all of the Evangelists and ministers who were ordained this day. We know that without your anointing, Lord, we can't do anything. Please take each of us to the place you have for us. I am so excited about the things God is doing in His people's lives.

November 11, 2011

Can you believe the date? November 11, 2011. We won't have this date—11/11/11—again. I am so excited. Today is the day I have my last round of chemo treatments. It started Wednesday. Today is Friday, and after the nurses take off the pump, I will be celebrating my last round of treatments. God is so good. George and Terry came with me to celebrate. My husband wanted to be there with me when I went through the graduation. The nurses gave me a graduation cap and took pictures of me with my husband, Terry and my special nurses. What a day this has been. I cried and cried. I can't believe I made it through each treatment. I am so happy. Though I still feel tired from the trip and nauseated from the chemo, I wanted to go somewhere to celebrate. I sent an email to my friends letting them know that today I would be celebrating my last treatment. I am so grateful to have so many people praying for me and supporting me through this. I am now waiting for the next step. God, thank you so much. Thank you for helping me keep a sound mind. I made it.

November 23, 2011

This is an event I will always remember. All my family was coming to Hampton to celebrate with me for Thanksgiving. Not only my family, but also my husband's sisters and their families. I was sitting, thinking about how great God is for blessing us with the finances to have such a big dinner. We were able to rent the Community Building at Lake Warren. I love that building and the area. The lake is so beautiful and the weather is outstanding. I know the dinner will be a lot of work and will cost a lot of money, but God has provided everything we need for the occasion. My brother helped me with the cost, and everyone is bringing a covered dish. Lord, I just want to thank you. I'm asking God to not let it be just another dinner, but a time to tell about His goodness. Let all of us see your grace and your mercy. Let all of us know how awesome you are. You have allowed me to go through 12 rounds of chemo and still be able to eat, still able to live. You have healed my body, and I want others to see your miracle. Nothing is too hard for you. Please bless this Thanksgiving meal and fellowship with my family.

November 24, 2011

Here it is Thanksgiving Day 2011 and I am so excited. My brother Tony and his family came down from Virginia on last night to celebrate with us and to cook. Tony and Ro blesses me every year by coming down and cooking Thanksgiving dinner. I am so proud of my only brother......my big brother. He and his wife don't mind working hard. This Thanksgiving is special because I asked all of my siblings and George siblings to come together with their families and celebrate together. Everyone is here today and others are on the way. I am so proud of my family. It is so good to see my sisters, Ann and Shirley, and my many nieces and nephews. After preparing all the food including the turkeys and ham, we backed up the car and headed to Lake Warren State Park Community Center. I love this place. It's in a perfect spot near the lake. The view of the Lake is magnificent. Everyone was coming in bringing their dishes. My nephew Dewayne cooked all the collards greens. He knows how to cook them like mom use to. Looking around you could see that we had enough food to feed an army. I am grateful that everyone did what they were supposed to do. We invited my mom's old neighbor from Allendale, Mrs. Josie Dupree. It's so good seeing her. She was one of mom's best friends and she was a great neighbor. My family loves her. My brother-in-law, Erol, bought down my favorite Jamaican food, curry chicken and jerk chicken. We had so many delicious desserts. I made banana pudding which my family loves. I am so happy to see everyone together. Wow, Lord thank you for allowing my family to come together. I had tears in my eyes all day seeing everyone smiling. Today I am grateful to cancer for bringing my family together. We had a little program before dinner. We sung some songs, prayed and my niece, Dee Dee, quoted our scripture for today. She quoted the entire scripture verbatim. I am so proud of her. We each shared why we were thankful and we cried a lot. My in-laws are awesome. There are always there for me. I am so glad we are together today..........Oh what a happy, happy, day!

December 6, 2011

Here I am now lying in bed crying and praying. Why, I don't know, but I do know that God is in control. When I want to be sad and down it seems I can't. I know the Lord will bring me out. He is right here now. God you have blessed me so very much. Let me enjoy my life while I'm here. Let the joy of the Lord be my strength. I need you so very much just to lead and guide me into all truth. I know my sons need salvation. Lord please help them become the men you have ordained them to be. Fill them with your precious Holy Ghost. I know one day my sons will have a relationship with you. Until that time, protect and guide them.

December 19, 2011

    My oncologist sent me to MUSC to meet with the surgeon who will be performing my liver surgery. I had to first have another CAT scan to see how much the tumors on my liver have shrunk and if he can now do the surgery to remove them. I was so disappointed when we walked out of the surgeon's office. I was told that not only do I have to go through another round of chemo, but he found another tumor on my liver, which now makes it three tumors instead of two. What do you mean another tumor, another round? Lord, you said I will not die but live and declare the works of the Lord. How can I do this… another 12 rounds of chemo? All I know to do is pray. Pray for God to strengthen not only my body, but my mind, too. I have to live what I tell others to do, which is to trust God with all of you. The question is, "what to do when you don't know what to do?" My answer today is, just believe in the promises of God. He said He would never leave me or forsake me. No, I do not want to go through chemo again. I hate to think about going through those treatments. Jesus is my hope. He knows chemo is not easy. He knows how much I hate going through it. I can't imagine going through these treatments without Him. I know the Lord will be there as He was during the last 12 treatments. Help me, Lord!

December 25, 2011

I am so blessed because one of my prayers was to take a family vacation with my three sons. Well, God answers prayers because this Christmas He allowed me and my family to go to Virginia Beach to be with my brother and his family for Christmas. God blessed us with the finances and everything we needed to have a wonderful time and to enjoy each other on the ride there and back. We stopped at Cracker Barrel in Walterboro to eat breakfast. It was so nice to have my sons and husband all together. Yes, I am very proud of my family. No, my sons are not perfect, but they are blessings from the Lord, and I love them. We all want the best for our children, so we have to continue to pray for each of them individually. Each of them are so different. I am proud to be with these men today having breakfast. We were able to rent an SUV for the five of us. It was an amazing trip. This was the best Christmas dinner I had since Mom died. My brother was blessed with my mother's gift of cooking. My brother and his wife are excellent host and hostess. They pampered us with lots of love and food. We were glad to be there. I know my sons missed their girlfriends, but I am truly grateful for their sacrifices to be with us. I will always remember this. My husband is such a wonderful man. He drove us to Virginia and back. He wanted his family to be safe. Continue to bless this man of God. He is such a wonderful, loving, caring man, and I am so grateful to have him as my husband.

1 Corinthians 13:4-7 (NKJV)

"Love suffers long and is kind; love does not envy; love does not parade itself, is not puffed up; does not behave rudely, does not seek its own, is not provoked, thinks no evil; does not rejoice in iniquity, but rejoices in the truth; bears all things, believes all things, hopes all things, endures all things."

December 29, 2011

I couldn't sleep, so I decided to write a little tonight. You can say it's my New Year letter declaring "Out with the old and in with the new." I was thinking about how my life has changed so much since May 10, 2011. I would have never thought it would be this way, but it is. So, what lessons have I learned from all of this? This is what I have learned: No matter how hard we try to plan or control our lives, each year all of us are faced with situations and circumstances that are completely out of our control. Many people entered this year very differently from the previous one. Some entered with disappointments, loss of work, or financial problems, while others faced the New Year fighting a sickness, missing a loved one, or without a home. At times like these, Jesus speaks to us just as he did to a father named Jairus when he found out his daughter had just died, "Don't be afraid. Just trust me." (Mark 5:36)

Looking back over the last few months, I have seen disappointments, I have seen friends who have passed away, and I have made poor decisions, but, in order for me to move forward, to continue growing, to continue reaching for a higher level, I had to put aside my poor decisions and past disappointments. Paul says, "We are pressed on every side by troubles, but we are not crushed and broken. We are perplexed, but we don't give up and quit. We are hunted down, but God never abandons us. We get knocked down, but we get up again and keep going, for our present troubles are quite small and don't last very long. Yet they produce for us an immeasurable great glory that will last forever!" (2 Corinthians 4:8-9, 17-18) Yes, I feel pressed on every side, but I know I must never give up.

As I was reading tonight, I found these words and I thought about myself: "Are you a student or are you a victim?" That's a great question. When hard times come, are you a student or a victim? The more I thought about these words, the more I thought about my situation.

Many people act like victims, always talking about how unfair life is. A victim says, "Why did this happen to me?" A student says, "I don't care why it happened. I want to learn what God is trying to teach me." A victim looks at everyone else and cries out, "Life isn't fair." A student looks at life and says, "What happened to me could have happened to anybody." A victim feels so sorry for himself that he has no time for others. A student focuses on helping others so that he has no time to feel sorry for himself. A victim begs God to remove the problems of life so that he might be happy. A student has learned through the problems of life that God alone is the source of all true happiness.

What a lesson to learn before this year ends and another one begins with all its problems and difficult situations.

January 4, 2012

All of us have a story. Some people look so happy that you think they don't have a care in the world. But how many know they do? Today, I want to encourage you with my story. Many people have secretly given up on God because they feel that He has forgotten them. To all those people, God says, "I am still here and I care about you."

All of us come to a breaking point. We come to moments that change the course of our lives forever. It's amazing how things can change so suddenly. So many things can happen so quickly. It may be like my story, when a few weeks ago, the doctor walked into the room and said, "You must go through another round of chemo." Time stops. How will I find the strength to go on? I came to a breaking point and I'm willing to admit it, but I thank God for His Word! To those people whose faith has come to a breaking point, know that God is still there.

When my oncologist came into his office, he looked at me and my husband and informed us that the first 12 rounds of chemo did not shrink the tumors on my liver enough for them to be removed. I was told that I had to go through at least another 12 rounds. Once I got over the shock of hearing this, I knew I had to ask God to strengthen me because I could not do this without Him. I was so disappointed, but I knew there was nothing more I could do. I was struggling because I was at a breaking point in my life. God, why? Why do I have to go through this again? I knew I had to believe that this time the chemo would work. But I didn't want it to be another time. I wanted this to end right now. I wanted the doctors to tell me that the tumors could be removed and that I would not die but live. The Word of God was my source of strength.

I came home and read Isaiah 40:28-29. I needed to remember God's promises: "He is the everlasting God. He is the Creator of the ends of the earth. He never grows weary. His understanding is unsearchable. He gives power to the faint, and to him who has no might he increases strength." God will supply strength in our weakness. He will strengthen us during our hard times. He will give us the power and ability to do what needs to be done. That's the way life is. Even the strongest of the strong lose heart and give way. No one can take the strain of life forever. But the good news is…God promises strength in our moment of weakness. And it arrives in the nick of time. Here, then, is the promise for all of us: "They that wait upon the Lord will renew their strength." (Isaiah 40:31) This is the promise of God.

January 17, 2012

Today I had my first treatment of Round 2 of chemo. I felt good when I came home, but later I couldn't sleep at all. I had a sleepless night. I may have slept two or three hours on and off, only to wake up feeling sick to my stomach. Around 7:00 a.m., I got up vomiting and feeling so bad. I can't believe I'm doing this again. I can't believe I have to go through chemo again. My heart hurts. I tried to be strong for my family, but right now, I just need to cry. George was right there in the bathroom with me with a cold washcloth for my head. God, please strengthen me. I need you right now to help me through every treatment, every blood test, every CAT scan. I can't do this without you, Lord. I need your help, and you promise to be my help in times of trouble. I know my God is able. I am depending on you. I don't have anyone else to turn to but you. I have found out when you're feeling low, just begin to praise God, and right now, I'm feeling very low. Praising God helps me think about Him and not what I'm going through right now. I was sitting on the floor beside my toilet and praising God. Can you only imagine how I felt and look right then? George was trying to hold back his tears and he was smiling at me, telling me it's going to be all right. I know it will, but when, Lord? I kept praising Him over and over again in my mind. Lord, I praise you.

January 19, 2012

I begin today thinking about what James says in James 1:2, "Consider it pure joy, my brothers, whenever you face trials of many kinds." James begins by reminding us that, sooner or later, we will all face trials of some sort. Life is like that for all of us. No matter who we are or where we live, trouble is just a phone call away. A doctor may say, "I'm sorry, but you have cancer." How should we respond to these hard times that suddenly come to us? James offers this advice: "Consider it pure joy." That sounds so crazy, right? How can we consider it pure joy? Are you nuts? Do you have any idea what I've just been through? Do you understand what I'm still going through? How can you tell me to consider it pure joy when my life is in an uproar?

I can't do it on my own, but what I have found out is that James was talking about a "supernatural joy" made possible only by the Holy Ghost, who enables us to see from God's eyes. It's a choice to see it this way and probably a choice we will have to make over again and again. I don't know about anyone else, but I choose to think like James and "consider it pure joy." I refuse to give in to my emotions or my feelings. I choose to believe and trust in God, who is my help and my strength. I will encourage myself and others to remember the Word of God during their trials and tribulations. I will pray and stay in His Word and hold on to my faith. God will see us through. He has promised.

February 1, 2012

Can you believe it's a new month and I have just completed the second treatment of Round 2 of chemo? I am very grateful that I don't feel like I did after my first treatment. Today I feel completely healed. I feel I had to go through the process for a purpose, not just for myself but for others, too. God is so good to me. He is forever faithful. I just pray to God that I learn and see the lessons from my trial. I read a sermon today that asked the question, "How does it look to you now?" I ask myself this question and realize that we really need to see ourselves as blessed, as God's Word has said to us. No matter what we are going through, we need to give God all the honor and all the praise. I know that's hard to do when you are going through, but it's the only way to go through. If I didn't have a relationship with God as I go through these trials, I would have, or should I say, I could have lost my mind. God is the one who promises me a sound mind. Yes, if it was not for the Lord on my side, tell me, where would I be?

Today my church family is sponsoring a benefit program for me and my family. I am so nervous and excited. I am excited about the people who will be participating. I feel really blessed that there are so many people who love me and my family. In spite of our problems, God still shows us His love through His people.

February 2, 2012

Yesterday was my benefit program which was so good. I can't believe the people who came to support me and my family. The church was totally packed. My brother came down from Virginia to surprise me. My co-workers from LeCreuset were there. So many people from Hampton County were there. So many pastors along with their members were there. My Sister2Sister group from Allendale came to support me. We felt so blessed. The program was outstanding. Co-Pastor Crystal did a great job organizing this event. Terry did the program and invited my special guests to speak and sing. They were all so amazing. I appreciate each person that came to say a few words or came to sing a song. Thanks to Robin Wright for blessing us with her gift. One of my guest speakers was our House of Representatives, Mr. Bill Bowers. I felt honored that he came and spoke on the program. My boss from LeCreuset, Mr. Archie Murdaugh and my sister-in-law Terry wrote amazing tributes to me that I will never forget. Needless to say I cried………

(Read Tributes beginning on page 192)

February 3, 2012

Many may wonder why I am sharing my testimony or why I am sharing what I am going through, but God uses our testimonies to give others hope and encouragement. Can your testimony give hope or encouragement that speaks to people and causes a desire in them to live better? If so, then that is a story worth telling. Revelation 12:11 says, "And they overcame him by the blood of the Lamb, and by the word of their testimony." Don't despise your testimony or the testimonies of others. Each test that God brings us through is another testimony of His power at work in our lives. God doesn't want us to waste our pain, but to use it for His glory, and that is why I share my story.

Life is a journey and it's not always easy. There are hard days and difficult nights and sometimes there are weeks and months where life seems to lead us from one hardship to another. No one is exempt from the troubles of the world. But the good news is that God promises never to leave us or forsake us. He is always faithful.

Life can be difficult. It's during those times that we ask, "God, why is this happening to me?" What happens if God remains silent? Is He listening? Is His faithfulness true? Well, I know that God is always faithful, even when you feel defeated or fearful. Even though you may not see Him, He has not abandoned you, and His faithfulness can be trusted. We never suffer alone. He says in Isaiah 41:10, "Fear not, for I am with you: be not dismayed, for I am your God: I will strengthen you; yes, I will help you; I will uphold you with my righteous right hand."

Someone else is always watching you. Our friends watch to see how we will respond to our problems. They want to know if what we say we believe is really enough for us during the hard times. Then there are those who are watching from a distance who don't believe in God. Many of them wonder if Christ is real. They don't know; they aren't sure. Maybe they've read the Bible or maybe they haven't, but they're watching how we respond to our situation, sickness, loss of a job, end of a marriage, and from behind, they watch God's people who are suffering to see if what they have is real or not.

There are many people in our lives who need our help. Some of them need a word of encouragement, and we are the only ones who can give them that word. Some of them have heavy loads, and some of them are about to quit, and we are the only ones who can keep them going. Those people are all around us, but we don't always see them. There are folks all around you who are just barely making it. You see them where you work and you may live next door to them. They are out there waiting for someone to give them help. And, through your testimony, you can help them. "We overcome by the word of our testimony." God has helped us for a purpose, so that we might take what we have received and share it with those who desperately need it. We have all been wounded and hurt with the burdens that weigh us down. Don't let your pain be wasted. Use it to grow closer to the Lord and to His people. Use it to minister to others. May God help us be an army of "wounded healers" who will take the comfort we have received in Jesus' name and offer it to a hurting world that is watching.

This is the Word of God that I needed to be reminded of. My pain is not going to be wasted. As I go through my rounds of chemo, I thank God for allowing me to share my pain with others. I can't believe I have made it this far. This fight has been one of the hardest things I have ever gone through. Yet, as I go back for my next treatment, I am reminded of Isaiah 41:10. God is my help, and I don't have to be afraid. I am not fighting this fight alone. God is with me and He has blessed me with a wonderful support team. I am truly blessed with a great husband and three wonderful sons, along with the rest of my family and friends. This fight has taught me about the power of love and sacrifice. Cancer is a terrible disease, but living through it teaches many valuable lessons that one might never have learned without it.

February 20, 2012
Love Without Limits

I just wanted to take this time to say thank you to all of those who supported me during my benefit program that was sponsored by my pastors, Jerome & Crystal Lewis, along with my church family at KTM, on Saturday, February 1, 2012. To those who have been there from the beginning, and even to those who couldn't come but supported me anyway, we are forever grateful for the love that was shown. How many know there is so much power in love? God's love has the power to restore, forgive, heal, and make whole. That's how I felt on that Saturday. I felt completely healed, restored and whole. It made me think, what if we became super lovers? What if we showed love like that every day? What would happen to our world? It made me think about Paul's prayer in I Thessalonians 3:12, which says, "May the Lord make your love increase and overflow for each other and for everyone else, just as ours does for you." That is an awesome prayer. Love without limits. You can never have too much of it. You can never have enough of it.

If we are full of God's love, it will overflow to others. It's not enough to be kind and polite. Our love must constantly be growing. How does that relate to their suffering? The answer is that when hard times come, we naturally start to pull away from other people and start focusing on our own problems. It's easy to become selfish, so that we only talk about our own struggles. Some people build walls in hard times to keep people away from them, while others build bridges so they can connect with God's people. I am so grateful that God has allowed me to connect with His people. I am so grateful that He has allowed me to love even in the midst of my struggles. I am so grateful that He has allowed me to be loved in my struggles.

Christian love is giving to others those things that you would want them to give you if you were in their situation— and doing so even if they can't pay you back. In fact, it's doing so especially if they can't pay you back! Christian love is respect for others. It's mercy. I encourage you all today to love without limits. "Love is the medicine for the sickness of the world." "Love cures. It cures those who give it and it cures those who receive it." I am a witness today that love cures.

It is the medicine we need in this sick world. I pray for you as you pray for me that we all can love without limits so that we all can be cured from all sicknesses. To live in love is to be like Jesus.

I have been blessed with so many people showing me love. So many friends are taking me to my chemo treatments, cooking dinner, and sending me cards with words of encouragement. I feel the power of love in my life right now, and it's just wonderful. Now I understand how love cures. God is touching the hearts of His people to show me Him. Oh, how very wonderful it feels. I never knew love like this. I am so very humble and grateful for these lessons I am learning on this journey. My life is even more wonderful than it has been. Is that possible? Yes, it is. I have gained so much from this experience, more than I would have ever thought possible.

Romans 12:10 (NKJV)

"Be kindly affectionate to one another with brotherly love, in honor giving preference to one another."

February 29, 2012

Here I am now after my fourth treatment of Round 2, which makes this my 16th treatment. God, help me go through this. For some reason, I am having a hard time dealing with this particular treatment. My blood pressure was up when I got to the doctor's office. I wanted to scream and run away from the Center, but I knew I couldn't. My last treatment wasn't so good either, and I guess I keep thinking about how nauseous I felt. Usually, after a few days I feel better, but, for some reason, I couldn't shake the nausea this day and stayed in bed longer. I didn't even go to church and, for me, the only reason I stay home from church is I'm too sick to go. I love going to the house of God because the words restore, revive and renew me so I can go a little bit further.

Now, here I am again, facing the same feeling. Who would be excited about going to get chemo? God give me your strength so I can go through this. I know there is a greater purpose for me to go through this process of healing. Help me to continue to fight, especially during the time when I feel like I can't go on. I can't give up now. Why should I feel discouraged? Why should I feel defeated? There is no reason I should be feeling this way, but there are times when the flesh gets weak. That's when I know I need to hear the Word of God more and more and more. That's what keeps me sane. Your wisdom, knowledge and understanding are what I need. Help me to understand this process and remember my purpose.

This is not for me, but for your glory. Let others know that they can make it, too, through Your Word. We can do all things through Christ Jesus. I know this is true. I'm a living witness. Though I am feeling bad, I thought about yesterday when the doctor looked at my blood work and said it was remarkable. My blood work was better this time than the last treatment. How can that be? My white blood count went up instead of down and my red blood count was higher than ever. I had to laugh at that. God is just amazing.

March 2, 2012
Can Suffering be Good for Us?

Is suffering good for us? I have been thinking about that question and wanted to share my answer. It's a question that each of us has to answer for ourselves. I have been thinking about this since going through chemo treatments and wondering, Lord, why do I have to go through the things I go through? I read this morning something I wrote in my journal on May 24, 2011. I wrote that cancer was a blessing in my life. You may wonder how I could consider finding out that I had Stage IV Colon Cancer a blessing in my life. Well, this is my answer...

May 10, 2011, was the day that I began learning about LIFE. This was the day that I began to learn the answer to the question, "Is suffering good for us?" Now I can answer. Yes, suffering can be good for us! This is what I have learned since that day..... to depend on God's grace, mercy and love in every area of my life; to put pride aside; that, by yourself, you fall and fail—that's why we need each other; that suffering takes you to the place where you discover how much you really need God; that most material things aren't much help when you are going through suffering; that it's a good thing to let down the walls and share with others what you are going through so it can help others; why the gospel of Jesus Christ is good news! God loves you and is with you! You're not out there on your own. When you have little to lose, you're freer to give yourself away; away to God and His Word, and away to others.

So, yes, friends, suffering can be good for us, especially when we learn the lessons God is trying to teach us. The spiritual lessons we gain from suffering don't come from what we're suffering; they come from the fact that God can take bad situations and make something good come out of them. He enjoys doing that! It is this that gives us real reason to hope during suffering. I know God is making it all good. As I go through each and every treatment, I am asking God, "What do you want me to learn today?" He is showing me His Word, which says, "I can do all things through Christ who strengthens me." (Philippians 4:13)

March 6, 2012

I was listening to T.D. Jakes this morning and he said, "God will allow people to like you for a season just to get you where He wants you to go." Wow! I don't know about some people in my life, but, Lord, mold me and help me forgive those things that people have done to me and have said about me. I do think about those scriptures in the Bible that say that I have done the same to others. I know I must forgive people so God will forgive me. Lord, please cleanse me. I know life may not seem fair. Help me to let go of all the pain and hurts of my past. Help me to not worry about what others think of me. This is my prayer for today.

March 14, 2012
Thank You

Gratitude is defined as a feeling of thankfulness or appreciation, and it describes what I felt as a result of the Basketball Benefit given in my honor on Saturday, March 10, 2012, at Hampton Elementary School by a wonderful group of women. The turnout for this event was amazing, and I just wanted to say thank you for your love, prayers and support. You have been there sharing your support during my good days and bad days. I truly thank each of you for your kindness and understanding. I know that "weeping may endure for a night, but joy comes in the morning." I am waiting for my morning. In the meantime, while I wait, I will praise God for great friends like all of you for helping me get through this.

Thanks Joyce Dunbar.

I also want to thank the players for participating in the games, along with the referees for officiating. I have to thank my own special cheerleaders, who worked hard over the last few weeks just to cheer for this event. Thank you, "Heat Cheerleaders." You were great! Again, thank each and everyone who came and the businesses that donated everything that was needed. Even for those who couldn't come to the event, but supported it, I say thank you. My heart is rejoicing to see the love and unity of Hampton County coming together to help others in their time of need.

I am determined to live. Jesus Christ is my strength, and I don't know what I would do without Him. Just know that your love and support are also a source of strength, and I thank each of you for that. I have to say thank you to my wonderful husband, George, and my sons, Jamel, Randy and Anthony, for their love and support. I am truly blessed to have a great family like you along with my church family at Kingdom Touch Ministries in Ridgeland, and all the other churches that have supported us.

I would like to also thank the following businesses for their support: LeCreuset of America, Scotsman, Nevamar, Sunoco, Accessnetwork, Subway, Hampton County Sheriff's Dept., Simply Soul Restaurant,

WDOG, WBHC, CDI, Hampton County Guardian, and Jimmy Denmark, along with so many others that I cannot name. Just know that God knows each of you by name and He will bless you for being a blessing to others.

It almost seems impossible to really give the thanks that I feel in my heart, but my husband and I have asked God that He "...supply all your needs according to his riches in glory by Christ Jesus," (Philippians 4:19) and that the sacrifices of your finances, time and love be returned to you one-hundredfold.

March 28, 2012

What a year, a month, a day I have had. Lord, I don't even know what to write about anymore. I want to just sit here and cry, but when I ask myself why, I can't seem to answer that. Every time I look at myself in the mirror, I know that because of God's grace and mercy, I am still here, and that I am truly blessed. Yes, Lord, I have asked you to take this cup away from me. Now I have had 18 rounds of chemo and I'm not looking forward to the rest of them. I want to stop right now, but I know I can't quit. Lord, please help me to understand my process. Yes, this experience has helped me to grow and to be more thankful. It has helped me to see who I really am in the Lord and the things that need to be changed in me. I know my life will never be the same again and, sometimes, that in itself is good.

So here is my prayer to you, God, for me and for others who are fighting for their lives: Doctors are giving fearful reports, but we hold to Your Word that never fails. We will have no fear in Jesus' Mighty Name, Amen. God, thank you, because you have not given a spirit of fear, but of power, of love and of a sound mind. We cast out every fearful thought from our minds and our hearts.

Thank you, God, for Your Word in Psalms 119:165: "Great peace have they which love thy law: and nothing shall offend them." Thank you again, God. Psalms 34:19 says, "Many are the afflictions of the righteous: but the LORD delivereth him out of them all." Yes, Lord, even though afflictions will come my way, I remain in peace in the assurance that you are Faithful and you will not allow that which is greater than what you have ordained me to carry. In Jesus' name, Amen.

April 3, 2012

Yesterday, we had to travel to Atlanta to see about our son, Randy, who totally lost his truck in a car accident. Though it happened on April 1, he just decided to call us to let us know about it. Lord, please help our son be more responsible for his actions. Please keep our children safe. Let me live to see my sons grow up to be men who are reliable, responsible, respectful, honorable, strong and, most of all, men of God who are able to take care of themselves and their families. Let them see, God, that you gave them a great role model in their own home while they were growing up. Their dad has been all of those things and more. He has been a great provider and protector of our family. I wish my sons knew how blessed they are to have a father like George. No, he's not perfect, but he has tried so hard to be the best dad for his sons. Thank you, God, for giving me a great husband and father of my children. I wish George knew how great he has been as a father. Right now he looks so disappointed and is wondering what he has done wrong as a dad. I don't know why we take all the responsibility for our children's actions upon our shoulders. They are adults, and though we teach them the right thing to do, they don't always listen. As I recall, we didn't listen to our parents either. Isn't that ironic? Every child is different, though, and I'm just praying that one day Randy will be a husband and father like his dad. I know he will. I believe he will.

Thanks, God.

April 5, 2012

Hello, God. What can I say about you today? I was interviewed by Michael Dewitt of the Hampton County Guardian newspaper today. He came out to my house. The interview lasted about two hours, and it was great. I was so happy to share my testimony with him. We talked about how I felt from the beginning until now. We talked about how I felt during the chemo treatments and how I felt after the treatments. It was a great interview. I am glad to be able to share my story with the world. I pray that it will help someone else. I can't wait to read it in the Guardian.

April 11, 2012
Nevertheless

I had no idea that my whole life was about to change…. again. That's usually how God works. We're just going on in life, business as usual, doing our thing, and suddenly the Lord comes in and redirects our steps. My experience has been that you can't predict this in advance. We never know when it will happen. If we did, we would try to change God's Will for our lives. As Jesus pointed out in John 3:8, the Spirit blows wherever it wishes. You never know when God's call will "launch you out into the deep." As of this week, I have endured 19 treatments of chemo. I feel as if I have been launched way out into the deep and am waiting to come back to land. I have been asking God to remove this bitter cup from my life as Jesus prayed in the garden, saying, "Father, if thou be willing, remove this cup from me: nevertheless not my will, but thine, be done." (Luke 22:42) I know that I, too, must say, "Nevertheless, Lord, let Your Will be done." Why? Because God's Will for our lives is always perfect. He planned our ending before our beginning. He'll move us from where we are to where He wants us to be. Things may start happening quickly. Things in our lives may not make sense but, nevertheless, we must know that God is working it out for our good. We must step out in faith and hope into the great nevertheless of God, trusting that God is leading us on, drawing us into His plan even when we cannot see the way. We may live in difficult times. Nevertheless, God is with us, guiding us into His promise. We do not see the hope that we hold to. Nevertheless, it is this hope that saves us and for which we are given the ability to endure. We may not know what God has in store for us. Nevertheless, the Spirit knows the mind of God and leads us toward the Will of the one who made us for His own purposes.

There is great power in nevertheless. This word can change the outcome of your life. It can be negative or positive. It's all in how you look at it. You can be obedient or disobedient to it. You can trust God at His Word or not. I know that, in my life, this is all a process to get me to the place of blessing He has in store for me. I may not see it; nevertheless, I choose to trust Him for it. Just know that there is power in nevertheless.

April 23, 2012
Open Doors

The Word of God lets us know that when God opens a door, no one can shut it, and when He closes a door, no one can open it. Sometimes people ask me, "How do you know when God has opened a door?" And my answer is, "You won't know until you go through the door." That's been my experience... that sometimes the door is obvious and we can just walk right through it. And sometimes we need someone to push us a little so we can go through it.

Open doors are like that. God rarely shows us the big picture in advance. The "open door" is usually a door pushed slightly open. We still have to have the courage to go through the door and see what's on the other side. It's a good thing that we don't know the future because we couldn't handle it. The future, with all its ups and downs, with all the unexpected things that we don't see coming, is so scary that if we knew what was coming, we would probably run the other way. I have found that life is better lived one day at a time.

Jesus, the one who has all authority, opens doors for His people. It's His job to open the doors. Our job is to go through the doors He opens, one step at a time, one foot in front of the other, going wherever He may lead us. One door may open, and then it may close. That's okay. Another door may open and then close. We may have to sit still for a while waiting for a door to open. That's okay.

All I know is that we can trust Him no matter what door He opens for us. He knows what's best for us. I came to that conclusion after finding out that I had to go through more chemo treatments; I'm now at my 20th treatment. I wanted this door to close, but it's still open and I have to, again, put one foot in front of the other and go wherever He may lead me.

Can I trust Him? Yes! Who else can I trust my life to? Who else can promise me that he will be with me, strengthen me, help me, and uphold me with his righteous right hand? Who else can promise to restore my health and heal my wounds? Who else but God? So don't be afraid to go through the doors that God has opened for you...

you can trust Him completely. I know because I am living testimony. I'm here today because of God's grace and mercy. I am no longer afraid to go through this door that He has opened for me. I have four more treatments and I know that God will strengthen me to go through each and every one of them one day at a time, one foot in front of the other.

April 26, 2012

Michael Dewitt's article appeared in the Hampton County Guardian today. It was a wonderful article and I thank Michael for it. I want to share it with you. For easier reading, I have adjusted the paragraphing, but here's the content just as the newspaper presented it.

'Diary of a Glad, Black Woman'

Liz Orr keeps a journal. A diary of triumphant hope in the face of cancer. She calls it, her 'Diary of a Glad Black Woman.' "By sharing, it helps me get my emotions out," says Orr. "That's been part of my therapy. And I hope to leave my diary to my kids one day."

Orr has responded to the news of her cancer in a unique and astounding way. "You don't know when life is going to end. This can be a good thing, this can make you think about life even more. Now I enjoy opening the door and looking at the sunshine and saying, 'Man, it's a beautiful day!' You notice the little things, you don't take that stuff for granted anymore."

"I choose to be happy, even in the midst of cancer, even going through this. It's the Lord. Even if you know you're going to die, you know it's going to be okay. I don't have anything to be sad about. I can be happy going through this, and I want to make everyone else happy."

Cancer has also brought Orr closer to her family: her husband, George, and sons, Randy, Jamel, and Anthony. "What a wonderful man I'm married to. We sometimes take our spouses for granted, and we shouldn't. I couldn't do this without my husband and family. My sons call me every day, and my brother and sisters are closer now than ever. Cancer brings the family closer."

A message of hope Orr, an evangelist, says she has been getting conflicting reports on her cancer status."I believe the doctor's report, but I have faith in the Lord's report. You have to have faith in the Lord's report; even though it's Stage 4 cancer, there is still hope. In Stage 4 you don't know what to expect, but no matter what's in the doctor's report I'm not going anywhere until the Lord is ready."

Some cancer patients become withdrawn and undergo their struggle privately. Not Orr. To express her feelings of hope, and to take her mind off her symptoms and the miserable chemo-therapy, she began writing words of inspiration and testimony and sharing them with listeners of Hampton and Allendale radio stations. She has a five-minute segment on the first and third Sunday on Cruise 92.1's "Pookie Smith Old School Gospel Show," which airs Sundays from 4 p.m. to 7 p.m. She also sends her words of hope via email to scores of friends, family, and former coworkers. She visits churches with her message, and was a key speaker at Huspah Baptist's Mother's Day program. "God allowed me to still be here for a purpose, and maybe it's to inspire."

A dark struggle.

But it hasn't always been easy to keep that optimistic smile. Cancer digs its claws into its victims in physical, emotional, and financial ways. Orr believes her cancer may have rooted and bloomed from too much stress. During the time she was diagnosed she was trying to work, go to college, raise a family, and care for her mother, who died of heart problems in 2009. She took care of everyone else. She neglected her own doctor appointments.

While undergoing gall bladder surgery later, doctors discovered Orr had full-blown Stage 4 colon cancer on May 10, 2011. Doctors had to remove a fourth of her colon, but the scourge had already spread to her liver. An initial round of chemo did not shrink all of the spots on her liver, and she is undergoing round two.

She had planned to be out of work for only eight weeks for the surgery, but no one can plan for cancer. Her employer, Le Creuset - one of the most active supporters of Relay in Hampton County - helped her as much and as long as they could, but eventually her health declined too much and the company had to replace her because of the vital essence of her job, payroll and wholesale accounting. The company had been her home and family since January 2002. Her Family and Medical Leave Act (FMLA) disability benefits ended on Dec. 31. "I just love Le Creuset, they've been good to me. They would have kept my job if they knew I was coming back. But I knew eventually I was going to lose my benefits.

While her husband had insurance through his employer, she has to maintain very costly COBRA (Consolidated Omnibus Budget Reconciliation Act) coverage. Orr searched everywhere for help, but was disappointed at every turn. Medicare said she had to wait two years. She was denied Medicaid because of her husband's income. Other government programs would provide insurance, after six months, during which time medical bills were mounting. Chemo costs between $10,000 and $12,000 per treatment. She needs two treatments a week. "The cost of treatment is unreal. They all say that help is out there, but I couldn't find much help. I called so many agencies, I even called the American Cancer Society."

Between bouts with chemo, and when not writing in her journal, Orr took it upon herself to write to state and federal officials to inform them of the struggles cancer patients endure. She wrote to Rep. Bill Bowers, Congressman Joe Wilson, and even the White House. Bowers and Wilson responded to her, but the White House forwarded her letter to Medicare.

She also found that suffering from colon cancer is unlike other diseases. Colon cancer is among the top five deadliest cancers, yet rarely talked about. "Many agencies have money for breast cancer, but not colon cancer ... Colon cancer is the most treatable cancer, but people aren't aware of it ... you hardly ever hear about colon cancer. Maybe it is embarrassing."

Orr urges everyone to remove stress from your life when possible, schedule a colonoscopy as recommended by your doctor and tell your doctor about any unusual long term symptoms such as acid reflux or chest and abdominal pain.

It takes a village.

Orr lives on a quiet, peaceful dirt road, Orr Road, surrounded by family. The sign that greets you says it all: Welcome to Orr Village. You get the impression this is a proud, close knit village that helps each other.

And when it comes to fighting cancer, Hampton County is much like Orr Village. When friends, neighbors, and even her former rec league soccer players - now adults - heard about her sickness, they came to her aid. Her co-workers take turns driving her to chemo in Charleston. And, thanks to them, bags of groceries keep magically appearing in the Orr kitchen. "I've had so much support, and this helps my husband tremendously. I haven't had the same person take me twice. They call it my "Chemo Calendar" and they all pass it around and fill it in. And my church family has been awesome."

Friends and family, like Lucille Kinard and Coretta Orr, have meals waiting on her and her husband when she returns, too sick to move. They began organizing fundraisers. Her pastor sponsored a benefit at Kingdom Touch Ministries in Ridgeland on Feb. 11. More than 400 attended, including S.C. Rep. Bill Bowers. A group of friends organized a March 10 basketball benefit at Hampton Elementary School.

An upcoming gospel singing benefit will be held May 26 at 5 p.m. at Happy Home Baptist Church in Allendale. Le Creuset and other local businesses donated items for the fundraisers. Employees at Nevamar passed the hat during one shift and collected $225 for Orr. People she doesn't even know sent cards. A friend in Country Acres sent her a doll baby. "That makes you excited. That makes me want to live, that makes me want to help others." In a perfect example of "paying it forward," Orr's son, Randy, a professional basketball player, sponsored an autographed jersey raffle at Hampton Elementary on March 30 and raised $900 for Victoria Tuten, a Hampton County teen also battling cancer. The Orr family also turned out to buy dinners during barbecue benefits held for Tuten.

"We live in the best community in the US of A. It's like a real family, we may talk about each other, but at the end of the day we love each other. When we need each other we know how to come together."

How will Orr's battle with cancer end? Such things are uncertain. Only the Lord knows, and he has yet to give his final report. But you can be sure of two things. Mrs. Liz will never give up hope and faith. And this beautiful woman is glad she lives in Hampton County.

Wow, this is great. Thank you, Michael, for a job well done.

May 1, 2012
How Much Time Do You Have Left?

How many know that time matters because, when time is gone, so is life? Therefore, what I do with the moments of my life—all of them—matters because sooner or later, for me and for you, time will be no more. Time matters because we have such a limited supply. How much time you have left, no one knows for sure. We live as if we have all the time in the world, but Psalm 90:12 says, "Teach us to number our days that we may gain a heart of wisdom." Have you ever numbered your days? That's hard to do because no one knows how many days he or she has left. But that's the point. Numbering our days keeps us from being foolish, thinking we will live forever and, therefore, giving excuses to put off doing what we know we should be doing. We have good intentions but somehow we never get around to carrying them out. We truly mean well; we mean for things to be different. We end up with the "ifs" of life: if I had done this or if I had done that. Some things need to be done now. The opportunity is today, not tomorrow.

Ephesians 5:16 reminds us to redeem the time, to make every minute count. Time can be used or wasted, but, either way, once used, it can never be regained. Most of us don't think we are going to die tomorrow and that's why we let time slide by. That's why we don't redeem the time. If you knew that today was the last day of your life, who would you call? What would you say? Who would you be kind to? Who would you forgive? What good deed would you do? Who would you pray for? What sin would you confess? What email would you send? What relationship would you restore? Who in your life would you stop putting off telling about Jesus? Whatever it is, do it now. If you intend to spend time with your children, do it now. If you intend to spend time with your parents, do it now. Things can change so quickly. Just one phone call and your life can change forever. Just one doctor's visit and life may never be the same again.

We always have plenty of time to do anything we want to do. As for me, my time belongs to God, and, therefore, how I spend my days matters. Someday I will answer for what I did or didn't do. The Bible reminds us in Ecclesiastes 3 that "There is a time for everything, A time for every purpose under the sun: A time to be born and a time to die; A time to plant and a time to uproot; A time to kill and a time to heal; A time to tear down and a time to build; A time to weep and a time to laugh; A time to mourn and a time to dance."

Today is an opportunity to hear from Christ. He is speaking to us today. He stands and knocks at the door of your heart. Will you open the door and let Him in? He says, "Come unto me, come now. Don't delay, don't put it off." Take today's opportunity. Every minute of your life counts.

Ephesians 5:15-20 (NKJV)

"See then that you walk circumspectly, not as fools but as wise, redeeming the time, because the days are evil. Therefore do not be unwise, but understand what the will of the Lord is. And do not be drunk with wine, in which is dissipation; but be filled with the Spirit, speaking to one another in psalms and hymns and spiritual songs, singing and making melody in your heart to the Lord, giving thanks always for all things to God the Father in the name of our Lord Jesus Christ."

May 11, 2012

God, what am I to do with the rest of my life? What am I doing wrong? Am I in the place that you want me to be? Am I walking in the right position? Where do you want me to be? Please let Your Will be done in my life. I sit here wondering why I'm back in this place of sorrow. Why do I feel trapped? That may not be the right word to describe how I feel right now, but I can't think of another word right now. I feel trapped in the condition that I don't want to be in. Lord, I'm asking you today for your strength. How much more do I have to endure? How much more do I have to suffer? I know right now I am feeling sorry for myself. Lord, like David, I ask you to restore me? Help me be joyful knowing that you are my strength and my salvation. I know I have to get my mind on what's coming ahead of me. I know, Lord, you are the same God who healed my body from my first surgery and I know you will do it again. I am asking that question again, "Why me?" Others tell me not to question you, but I don't know anyone else who can answer that question. I don't understand, Lord, what you are doing in my life, but you didn't ask us to understand, but to trust. Help me to trust you with my whole heart, Lord. Let me not secretly have doubt in my heart. I surrender all of my secret thoughts to you today. I repent of all unbelief that may be in my heart. I'm trusting you with my entire life. My life is in your hands. I will trust and obey Your Word. I will praise you with everything in me. I know everything will be well with my soul. I love you, Lord. Keep me in your path. I know that I will be healed in Jesus' name.

May 23, 2012
Round 2

Here it is the day before my second round of surgery. Tomorrow, I will be having surgery to remove three tumors from my liver. Last year, on May 10, 2011, while performing gallbladder surgery, doctors found tumors on my liver. I was informed later that week that I would be taking 12 rounds of chemo to shrink the tumors so they could be removed. Unfortunately for me, the first round did not shrink the tumors and I had to go through nine more rounds of chemo, which meant a total of 21 rounds. The second round worked, and the tumors were now small enough to be removed. At least that is what the doctors said. Thank God! All four of my doctors said that surgery on my liver would be best for me at this point. I am in no way looking forward to this day, but I do want to live and I know the same God that brought me through my first surgery and 21 chemo treatments will bring me through this. Yes, I am afraid of the unknown, but I know that I can trust God with my life because it was He who gave it to me in the first place.

I was waiting for my husband to get off work at noon. Our plan was to spend the night in Charleston because we had to be there at 6:30 a.m. My brother and sons were meeting us there that night at the Army base. I was so grateful that my brother was able to get us rooms at the base; that was one less thing I had to take care of. I would not eat after 12:00 p.m. that day so I made sure I had a good breakfast. It was hard not to eat any more that day. After George came home, we got ready to go to Charleston to meet up with my brother. My friends and family called that day to encourage me. It is a blessing to have a great family and friends. I knew everyone would be praying for me. It's hard to explain what I am feeling right now. Lord, I do want to live, but why do I have to go through another surgery? My husband is my greatest encourager. I know he wants me to live, and so do I.

My doctor is to remove 70% of my liver—all of the right side and 20% of the left side. Can I live like this? My doctors were giving me no hope if I did not have the surgery. What choice do I have? Once again I am asking why.....why must I go through another surgery? God, I know that if you just speak the word, my body will be healed. Why must I go through this process? Lord, I know you are in control of my life and I can trust you with all of me. I know you will never leave me. I know you will anoint the hands of the doctors and guide their every move. I know that you will give my family peace as they wait for the doctor's report. I know I can go through this liver surgery and I will live. God, again, show me your strength.

Psalm 23:4-6 (NKJV)

*"Yea, though I walk through the valley of the shadow of death,
I will fear no evil; for You are with me; Your rod and Your staff,
they comfort me. You prepare a table before me in the presence
of my enemies; You anoint my head with oil; My cup runs over.
Surely goodness and mercy shall follow me all the days of my life;
and I will dwell in the house of the Lord forever."*

May 24, 2012
Second Surgery

    I will never forget this day. This was a day of great faith. I underwent my second surgery—this time, to remove three cancerous tumors from my liver. The doctor was going to remove 70% of my liver. I was told that I would probably be in the hospital about four to six days. Yes, God was my only hope. I had so many family and friends with me that day. My husband, sons, sisters-in-law, brother, nephew and friends were there to support me. I know it was only by the grace of God that I came out of this. All I remember of this day is going into the surgery room. I woke up four days later.

May 29, 2012

I didn't wake up until four days after the surgery. I can't tell you what happened after surgery. I heard many stories from my husband, pastor, and family members who came to see me during those days. My husband told me that every day he tried to wake me up so I could eat. He told me I talked out of my head. He tried to give me ice to eat, but I refused it. The doctors told him if I didn't eat soon, they would have to put a feeding tube in me. I learned from my husband that I tried to get out of bed and, as a result, the IV in my neck came out. He had to call for the nurse, and I had two stitches put in my neck. There are so many stories I heard from my family. Have you ever had days that you missed in your life? It was like I was in a coma. No, the doctors didn't call it that, but it sounded like it.

I am so glad that my faith is in the Lord and not in the doctors. God said I would not die but live. I'm glad I believed the report of the Lord. I do understand that during this process so much could have happened. Actually, a lot did happen, but God brought me through each and every thing. I am so grateful to my God. He is my strength. Only with God's strength I survived all that happened to me. I am so glad I can count on Him 24/7. God is always there to answer your call. God is faithful and true. Believe in His promises. He promised me that I would not die but live. He never promised me that it would be easy. All I know is that I survived yet another surgery.

It wasn't easy at all. The four to six days I was supposed to stay to recover turned into 21 days. Yes, 21 days I spent at MUSC. The doctors told me I had an infection and they could not find where it was. All the doctors knew was that my white blood cell count was up and they didn't know why. They gave me three different antibiotics to destroy the infection. The antibiotics destroyed my taste buds. I couldn't eat or taste any food. I could only drink orange juice or cranberry juice. The doctors told my husband to bring in any food I would eat. That didn't work either. I don't know why, but I lost my appetite. I did not eat for two weeks. My nutrient levels hit rock bottom. The doctors told my husband that I had to eat to get better, that my body could not heal without food. Because I am a Type 2 diabetic,

I was given insulin—for the first time in my life. I was given 40 units at night and 10 units after each meal during the day even though I wasn't eating. For some reason, my blood sugar was higher than usual. I had fluid building up in my body and I had to have a tube inserted to remove some of it. Yes, here was something else to go through. I had two CAT scans in one week and the dye went to my kidneys, and now they were trying to shut down. My heart felt like it was skipping beats. The devil thought he had me, but God said I will not die but live.

I couldn't believe the things that happened in those 21 days. I had test after test to find out why I had an infection. They couldn't find anything. On top of this, I had a burn on my left leg and another on my right thigh from the surgery. How did that happen? Only God knows. I am now asking God why I had to go through the things I went through. When will these things end?

I stopped talking. I didn't want to say anything out loud that would sound like doubt. Nothing good would have come out of my mouth at that time so I remained quiet. I knew God's Word says that life and death are in the power of your tongue, so I didn't say a word. I knew that I just had to wait for God.

June 1, 2012

My husband asked me many times why I wasn't talking. I was beginning to get so weak. I couldn't hold my Bible, or even my cell phone, in my hands. I am so glad that the Word of God is inside me. All I could do each day was meditate on God's Word. My husband read the Bible to me at times. He tried so hard to keep me encouraged. He thought I was giving up, but all I could do was focus on God's promises. I didn't want to talk. I did listen to my husband and others who came to encourage me. I am so grateful to have family and friends who love me. Lord, when will these things end?

Every day the doctors would read my chart and do more tests. I had shots several times a day to prevent blood clots. I hated every needle. I hated being in the hospital. I hated going through so much, but I knew it was just part of the process of healing. I asked God, "Why not just speak Your Word right now and take this away from me?" He chose to allow me to go through these things for His glory. He wanted me to have a testimony to share with others that God is still a healer. I didn't know if I would leave that hospital, but I did know that, like Paul, whether I lived or died, I would still be with the Lord.

I am so grateful God allowed me to live. I want others to know that they can make it. I know they can. I am living testimony that God is able to bring you out no matter how bad it looks. The doctors had no answer as to why I had an infection; they could never find where it was. My white blood cell count just started going back down and my kidney and liver numbers were getting better.

I still couldn't eat, but the doctors thought maybe if I got in my home environment, things would turn around. It was as if they were saying just let her go home and die. There were days and nights I thought I would. One night George called our pastor and told him that he didn't think I would make it. My pastors came from Ridgeland late that night to pray for me and declare that I would not die but live. I am so glad I have leaders that believe in the power of prayer. George also called on other prayer warriors who prayed for me. Prayers of the righteous availeth much. I know prayer works. I am so glad for people who don't mind praying for others. God sent so many people to pray for me while I was in the hospital. Even the nurse sent someone to talk to me to make sure I would not fall into a state of depression. After talking to her only once, she said I would be okay. She saw the love that was being poured out on me by my family and friends, and she knew that my strength was coming from the Lord. I told her that God was going to heal me and I knew I would live. I was just asking Him for the strength to go through. We talked for an hour and I never saw her again.

Whenever my spirits were low, God sent someone there to remind me of His promises and His love for me. God also sent others there to be a blessing to my husband. They understood that he needed someone there for him, too. God is so amazing. He puts people in your life for a reason, a season or a lifetime. I really believe that. Some people came just for that season, and we so much appreciate all that they did. We had all the support anyone could ask for. People were there for our every need. God will supply all we need and He uses people to do it.

June 14, 2012

Finally, after 21 days, the doctors told me I could go home this morning. That was wonderful news even though my nutrient levels were at rock bottom and fluid was in every part of my body. I now weighed over 300 pounds because of the fluid throughout my body. George went home a few days ago because he had to go back to work, so he didn't know how much more weight I have gained because of the fluid. No one knew but me and my son, Randy, who stayed with me that week. We wanted to surprise George with my coming home, but after Randy posted it on Facebook, we decided to call and tell him before someone else did. He was so happy, and called everyone to tell them the news.

The doctors came in very early this morning to check on me and to say that they were releasing me. We waited and waited, but my release papers did not come in the morning. I prayed, "Lord, please let them just send me home." Though my body was hurting and I felt terrible, I still wanted to be home. Sometimes the hospital seems to make you worse instead of better. I was getting upset because I thought the doctors had changed their minds. I just kept praying, "Please, Lord, let them send me home." Finally, they released me at 5:00 p.m. I was so glad.

I didn't realize how much weight I had gained until I tried to get dressed to go home. My clothes didn't fit me. My shoes didn't fit me. I didn't care because I wanted to go home so badly. I put socks on my feet and made my skirt fit by stretching the elastic. I had to put on two shirts; one was too tight and the other was just to cover me. I looked like a mess but, again, I didn't care because I was going home. The nurses finally came to give me my orders and my insulin, along with pain pills, stool softener, and other medicine that I can't even remember; I just know that my bag was totally filled with medicine. Randy loaded me, my medicine, and other things in the truck, and we headed to Hampton.

When we arrived home, George met us outside. He was totally amazed at what he saw. He hadn't seen me for a few days and those days had made a big difference. He just smiled like he didn't notice my weight gain. He had to almost pick me up out of the truck to stand me at my walker so I could walk into the house. He told me later that he couldn't believe how much weight I had gained in those few days. I was miserable, but I was home. I knew I looked terrible, but I tried not to think about it because, at that point, all I wanted was to be with my family.

The doctors could not give me any answers. They didn't know what to say but "take care." They told me to call my family doctor as soon as I got home. I left MUSC not walking on my own, but using a walker. I went in one way and came out not knowing if I would live from one day to the next. Someone will have to help take care of me like a baby. I could no longer walk on my own. I couldn't go to the restroom on my own. I felt helpless but, still, happy to be home.

June 15, 2012

I knew that the road of recovery was not going to be easy. I was in so much pain but didn't want to take my pain pills; I hated the way they made me feel. I just stayed in bed and suffered. I felt completely helpless. Another reason I didn't want to take my pain pills is because I didn't want anything to control my mind but the Word of God. The pills make me sleep for hours and when I woke up, I begin to see colors and things on the wall. All I know is that I didn't want anything controlling my mind. I wanted my mind to be on the Word of God only, so I suffered the pain. I prayed and asked God to release me from the pain. If I have to go through this process, I wanted to do it without so much pain and without taking the pain medicine. I can no longer take care of myself. God, please help me. God, please heal me. You promised me that I would live. Let your promise be manifested right now.

Someone brought us dinner and I ate a little. When it was time to take some of my medication, we had to call a friend to help us. This was the first time I had to give myself a shot of insulin and I was scared I would overdose. Our friend, Val, came and called the nurse, who instructed us on how to give the shot of insulin. It was not a wonderful experience, but we did it. Later, as George slept, I cried and cried. I looked up at the ceiling and cried out to God. I know He was there. I know He heard me. He just wants me to trust Him. He promised to bring me through. Still, I can't help thinking, "Lord, how am I going to make it?"

The things I've had to go through have not been easy. I can't wait until each day is over because I know God will be healing me a little each day. I think about His promise that "weeping may endure for a night but joy comes in the morning." (Psalms 30:5) I'm waiting for my morning. I've heard my pastor say that it's only 60 seconds between night and morning. I'm waiting and walking it out each day.

Every day I try to walk so I can push some of the fluid through my veins. My legs and feet look as if they will burst at any time. I can only wear socks because my feet are so big. None of my clothes fit me now.

Several friends have purchased big house dresses that fit around me. I am miserable. I hate to even look at myself in the mirror. Because of the medication, I have dark pimples on my face. I have been dealing with rashes on my face, neck and throat from the chemo, and now I have even more dark spots. As I (I should say, as my sister) washes my face each day, I look at myself and cry. Wow, I can't believe what I'm seeing. I am not a conceited person. I have never thought of myself as being a beautiful woman, but I also have never considered myself ugly. Now, I felt ugly for the first time in my life.

I've had a lot of first experiences that I have hated. Hate is the only word to describe my feelings about the experiences. But I also know that I want to live and that those things, too, will pass sooner or later. I'm still waiting for my morning. In the meantime, once again I ask, "Lord, what am I to do?" Again, I hear, "Just wait for me."

July 16, 2012

Lord, why is this so hard? I'm trying every day to get better even when it seems like I'm not. I want to be well and be able to take care of myself. People are treating me like I'm lazy and not even trying to get out of this state I'm in right now. They don't understand how my body feels on the inside. Every day I feel so much pain in my body all day long. I'm trying hard to deal with it, but, Lord, if it had not been for you on my side, where would I be? I would have given up a long time ago. I would have given in to all the pain and hurt I'm feeling now. I know I would have lost my mind by now.

I'm not sure what my family is thinking, but if only they knew what's on my mind these days. It's been a long time since my surgery and I know my family thinks things should be better. I thought things would be better by now, too, but I'm still hurting and have so much fluid in my body. But guess what! It's not over yet, and I get up each and every morning and thank God for another day. Then I watch the time on the clock, waiting for another day to come. That may sound sad, but that is what I do every day—wait for each day to end so another one will start. Then this nightmare will be over.

I want to get up and not feel this pain, and not look the way I do. I'm not stuck on my looks, but I know this is not what I look like. Twenty-five years ago, I lost my hair to alopecia and felt completely ugly, and now I have spots on my face, and my body looks like a balloon.

How much can a person handle? That is the question I want someone to answer for me. How much must I go through? I know I can't stay in this dark place too long. I can't let it consume my thoughts. I'm still believing and I am still praying. Sometimes it's hard to keep believing. This is one of those days.

August 1, 2012

I find myself not writing in my journal as much. I was thinking about my reason for not writing and it's because every day seems like the day before and nothing is changing. I know things are happening but, in my mind, it's the same things happening every day.

My sister comes to my house every morning by 8:30 or 9:00 a.m. She helps me out of bed, washes me, and helps me get dressed. She prepares breakfast for me and I try to eat. The rest of day I am sitting and watching the clock, waiting for the day to be over. George comes home and makes me walk down the road to help get the fluid off my body. He pushes me so much, but I know he is just trying to help. I see that the fluid is leaving my body but there is so much more that is going on in my body. Help me understand, Lord. Help me to hold on to your promise that, "I shall not die but live and declare the works of the Lord." (Psalms 118:17) Help me fight that good fight of faith that I know is in me. I am learning how you have to encourage yourself. I know I have to keep fighting. I know that I have already won because I am still living. Yes, after two major surgeries and I can't remember how many chemo treatments, I am still among the living.

I know how blessed I am. I am blessed to have so many people praying for me and supporting and loving me. I am blessed to have a husband who is standing with me through all of this. I am blessed to have my sons help their dad take care of me. I am blessed to have my sisters here helping me every day. I am blessed to have an amazing nurse take care of me. I will make it, and things are going to get better. I am declaring this in Jesus' name. Today I am going to change my approach. Today I am going to stay in the battle and refuse to lose. Today I am determined to live and live life more abundantly. I am going to live in good health even when it doesn't look like it and in good spirit even when I don't feel like it. Today I refuse to lose this battle. Things will get better...I can see it now.

August 02, 2012

There is a story behind my praise. I am going through something but I'm not dead. I know I have to change my approach. I got to refuse to lose. I keep telling myself, I refuse to lose; I refuse to die; I am determined to live. I will live a life of abundance-----in good health when it doesn't look like it; in good spirit even when I don't feel like it. I know the Lord have strengthen me if though I feel weak. I keep telling myself I can make it even when it seems like I can't. Let's face it, sometimes we lose things. We lose our joy and end up anger. We lose our peace and end up worrying, but the good news is though we have lost some battles we are still victorious because Jesus has already paid the price for all of us. Our victory is in Him. When we are on the Lord's side we are in a place when we never lose. If God is for me, who can be against me? Losing is just not an option with God on your side. Thank you Lord for the VICTORY!

August 30, 2012

Today I was mediating on Psalm 107. I am so glad I am redeemed. Psalm 107 says, "O give thanks unto the Lord, for He is good and His mercy endureth forever. Let the redeemed of the Lord say so, whom he hath redeemed from the hand of the enemy; and gathered them out of the lands, from the east, and from the west, from the north and from the south."

There is a song by Israel Houghton I love to listen to. I love the lyrics of this song. The words to it says:

Let the redeemed of the Lord say so
Say So! Say So!

What does it mean to be saved?
Isn't it more than just a prayer to pray?
More than just a way to heaven?
What does it mean to be His?
To be formed in His likeness
Know that we have a purpose.

September 1, 2012

Things have changed so much. I am feeling so much better each day. I haven't been writing like I used to, but I have been reading more. My life won't ever be the same. God has shown me so much. As I think about those 21 days I stayed in the hospital, I realize there was a purpose.

I am just so grateful I am still alive. I can now take care of myself.

I went to church for the firsttime after my surgery and it was wonderful. We were late because I can't move as fast as before. When we arrived, Pastor Lewis was already up preaching, and when we entered the church, he stopped preaching and everyone stood up and applauded. It was something else. God is so good to us even when we don't seem to understand where He is leading us. God is so amazing. I was so happy to be back in the house of God. The spirit of the Lord was in that place and I felt God's Holy Spirit all over me. I was so happy.

I still have a long road ahead of me. Some fluid is still in my body and the doctor is going to do a procedure to take it off soon. In the meantime, I will just wear the bigger shirts and keep living. I can't believe how far I have come. I haven't had a CAT scan since my surgery. I am praying that the cancer is gone. All I can do is pray. Lord, please take this away from me.

I am so blessed and humbled by what I have learned. My life is more wonderful than before. I have gained so much more living with cancer than living without it, and I am so grateful. This may sound crazy, but it makes perfectly good sense to me. God has a purpose and a plan for our lives. He is always at work making us more like His Son. God can work all things out for our good.

September 15, 2012

This is what I learned today. This is how we overcome. My question today is how to be an overcomer? That's a great question and one I needed to know the answer to. Revelation 12:11 says that we overcome by the blood of the Lamb and the words of our testimony. The blood of Christ is the most powerful weapon in our lives, but it is only beneficial to us if we apply it to our lives. Today I apply the blood of Jesus on cancer in my body. I will be healed and set free. I believe in a miracle and I know it will come. I don't know when and I don't know how, but I believe by faith that I am an overcomer!

September 28, 2012

Have you ever wondered about waiting? None of us likes to wait. I'm here waiting for my miracle, and it's been so hard. To think about it, we don't like waiting at a doctor's office or waiting in line at the grocery store. Waiting is one of the hardest parts of our lives. What do we do while we wait? We all spend a part of our lives waiting for something to happen. My question today is what do we do in the meantime, while we wait? God told us over and over again in the Bible to wait. In Psalms 27:14 he says, "Wait for the Lord, be strong and take heart and wait for the Lord. My favorite scripture, Isaiah 40:31, says "They that wait upon the Lord shall renew their strength; they shall mount up with wings as eagles; they shall run, and not be weary; and they shall walk, and not faint." God told us to wait but He never told us how long to wait. We have no idea whether we should wait a week, a month, or a year. Some people have been waiting for 20 years or more for their prayers to be answered. How much longer can we wait for our healing, for our deliverance, for our dreams to come true? There are times when I feel like giving up and walking away but when I think about my family, my life, I continue to wait. I believe with all my heart that Jesus will heal me and set me free from this disease. No, I don't know when and I don't know how He is going to do it, but I believe by faith He will. In the meantime, Lord, I ask you to strengthen me and help me hold on to your promises. Are you willing to wait for God even if it takes forever? Yes, Lord, I will wait.

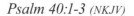

Psalm 40:1-3 (NKJV)

"I waited patiently of the Lord; and He inclined to me, and heard my cry. He also brought me up out of a horrible pit, Out of the miry clay, and set my feet upon a rock, and established my steps. He has put a new song in my mouth—Praise to our God; many will see it and fear, and will trust in the Lord."

October 1, 2012

My body is slowly healing from the surgery. I'm feeling better each day. Much of the fluid has left my body except in my stomach. Dr. Steigler told me he would set up a procedure to take the fluid from my abdomen. The fluid is there because of the liver trying to heal. I look like I'm three months pregnant. My legs and arms and the rest of my body seems to be free of fluid. I had to purchase more clothes just to fit around my belly. The problem is when I buy large-sized shirts, they are falling from my neck. I have been looking for maternity clothes. That's sad, but they seem to fit my body better. I'm not looking forward to going back to the hospital to get this done, but I know I really need it. It really seems like I'm pregnant. My back is even hurting now. I'm praying every day for all the cancer to be gone from my body. After going through this surgery, I pray that I never have to do this again. That surgery was very hard on my body, and I know if it had not been for God's grace and mercy I would not be here.

When I think back, how far I have come!

I'm so grateful for Dr. Shealy and Dr. Steigler, and Dr. Holladay, who have helped me so much. I can't say enough about my home health nurse, Jill Knight. She is a saint. She was so compassionate and loving and patient. She did so much for me and encouraged me to live. My sisters, Gloria and Linda, who took great care of me when I came home from the hospital, were life savers. I don't know what George and I would have done without them.

My husband, who is my caregiver, has shown me the true meaning of love. He has taken his wedding vows seriously. He has loved me through sickness and health. When I think back during the time of my surgery, I can see how much Jesus has done for me. God is so amazing. What would I have done without Him? Lord, today I want to thank you for bringing me this far. Today I am thanking God for all of His many blessings.

October 9, 2012

I had an appointment with Dr. Steigler for a checkup and to set up the procedure to take the fluid from my stomach. The procedure is called guided paracentesis and will be done at Colleton Regional Hospital. I don't know what to expect, but I'm so glad to be getting it done. It seems that the fluid will not go out of my stomach without help. Dr. Steigler explained to me that during paracentesis, a special needle punctures the stomach and the doctor is careful not to hit any organs. Glad to know that. The nurse at the hospital will do an ultrasound to find the best place to puncture the stomach. The procedure is set up for next week. I am still trusting God in all matters. I know this is for my good and it will help relieve the pressure on my back and stomach. I'm just ready to get this done. The weight from the fluid feels like I'm nine months pregnant. I'm even walking like I'm pregnant. I know this, too, shall pass. God, I'm calling on you again.

October 17, 2012

Today I had my parencentesis procedure. I had to go to Colleton Medical Center in Walterboro to get the proccdurc done. We went to go to the hospital early for blood tests and to complete registration. I was very nervous because I didn't know what to expect. After getting registered, I sat and waited for them to call me. I was glad I had pre-registered the week before. Of, course, the hospital wants your co-pay before they will do the procedure, but they did work with me and allowed me to make payments.

Dr. Steigler did well explaining the procedure to me, but, because so much has happened to my body, I was still afraid. The nurse who pre-registered me told me not to eat or drink prior to the procedure and to make sure I had a driver with me. Crystal came from Ridgeland to take me to the hospital. I am grateful for loving pastors. After the nurse called me, the first thing I had done was blood work. The nurses were so very nice. I found out the nurse who took my blood was related to my cousin-in- law, Darlene Boles. It's a small world. Then they sent me to another department and I waited until the nurse called me into a room. The nurse came in to explain what she was going to do first, before the doctor came in. After reading my doctor's record, the nurse talked to me about my cancer diagnosis. She couldn't believe what I had gone through. She was very sympathetic and caring. I thank God for good nurses. I can't remember my nurse's name; I wish I could. She first did a guided ultrasound to see the fluid in my stomach and then to see the best place to enter my stomach to drain the fluid out. She was so compassionate and gentle with me. She held my hand the entire time that she was doing the procedure.

After another nurse pinpointed the right spot to put the needle in, she went to get the doctor. The doctor came in, introduced himself, and explained what he was about to do. Help me, Lord. I cried when they put the needle into me. It hurt, and I could feel the suction from whatever they were using to remove the fluid. I didn't look to see what they were doing. All I know is that it hurt. After removing the fluid, the nurse pulled the needle and suction tube out. I did feel it and, yes, it did hurt. I felt so sore after it was removed. I had to wait a few minutes before getting off the table to make sure I was okay. I didn't feel weak, but I did feel so sore.

Believe it or not, they drained eight liters of fluid from my stomach. I couldn't believe that much fluid was in my belly and surrounding areas. Crystal took a picture of one of the liters to send to my husband. I asked if eight liters was a hospital record and the nurses said no. They told me the most they had experienced was nine liters, so I was a close second. My stomach was finally flat again. I think I lost 10 pounds that day. The procedure was not fun at all.

We waited a few minutes before leaving and then off we went. I was so glad to get that over with. I couldn't wait to call George to let him know how many liters were removed and how skinny I now looked. He wanted me to send him the picture Crystal took, but I didn't. I wanted to surprise him when he got home. Though I was very sore, I was so glad to have the procedure done. Thank you, God, for always being there with me and strengthening me through all things.

November 1, 2012

How many of us have asked the "what-if" questions in our minds? What if I get cancer? What if I get in a car accident? What if my husband or my wife leaves me? What if one of my children dies? What if I lose my job? What if I lose my house or my car? All of this and much more can bring on heart trouble. Everyone seems to have heart trouble these days. I was thinking about God's word in John 14:1, "Do not let your heart be troubled." This scripture is not just for funerals, but is a commandment from God for us to trust Him no matter what is going on in this world and in our lives. Lord, help me trust you with my life. I don't need any heart trouble.

November 18, 2012

I haven't written in my journal for a while. I don't know why. I had, and have, plenty of time to do it, but it hasn't seemed important like it used to. It seems each day is the same, so why write about it? The same thing is happening each day. It doesn't matter how I feel. Reality sets in after a while. I'm not saying I'm losing faith because, without it, I can't please God. I do trust God with my life. I guess I just want to know what is going to happen and when it will happen.

I haven't had a CAT scan since my liver surgery on the 24th of May. I'll be glad when that happens. I'm ready to do it. I know my test will be good. My body feels good. I get a little tired at times; my feet are freezing right now; and I have lots of gas pains; other than that, I feel blessed to be alive. Yesterday I found something that was not normal and I was scared, but I'm leaving that to God. Yes, I was scared and wanted to cry, but the spirit of the Lord blessed me with peace.

I'm so peaceful about what's going on inside of me. I know what God has promised me. He promised that I shall not die but live and declare the works of the Lord. Well, God, I want to live with good health and a sound mind and be able to take care of myself. Lord, help me be a living testimony, one that will glorify you. In my mind I want to say and do so much to help others, but why do I feel that all I'm supposed to do is just live? I'm supposed to just live and live with a smile on my face. Help me do that, Lord. Help me to live life to the fullest and in abundance.

November 22, 2012
Why?

Have you ever asked that question before? Why do bad things happen to some and not to others? There are many mysteries in life. The word of God tells us that "the secret things belong to the Lord our God," which means He knows why everything happens; why bad things happen to some and not others. In our lives today we may ask such questions as why one woman gets cancer at 18 and another one lives to be 90; why one man dies in a car accident and another walks away with only bruises; why one child does well in school and another one struggles; why one man is promoted when another is laid off; why some prayers are answered and some will never be. These are mysteries of life. Where do we find the answers to such questions? Psalms 115:3 says, "Our God is in heaven: He does whatever pleases Him."

In the last few weeks we have been hearing and seeing reports about Hurricane Sandy. We have watched the scenes on news reports that show great disaster, loss of homes, and even death. Why one home is destroyed, and the one next door has little damage? Why does one man die and another lives? Why did the storm go east and not west? It's natural for us to ask why. I, myself, have asked that question many times, especially, since May 10, 2011: Lord, why me?

November 29, 2012

I wanted to write each of my friends at LeCcreuset a personal letter for Christmas. Actually, I started writing the letters today. I knew it's a little early to write them, but I wanted to do it while I had it on my mind. I will see each of them for the Christmas dinner at Elaine's house. Today I am writing to Terry, who does not work at LeCreuset; she's my sister-in-law and she is also a part of the group with my friends from LeCreuset. I think this letter is good, and I wanted to start with Terry because she is my little sister. It's from my heart and I hope she will feel that. I am using each person's name and associating characteristics of Jesus Christ to describe who they are to me. These are the words I am using to describe Terry in my letter to her:

T – Teacher – Do you know the qualifications of being a good teacher in the Word of God? Well the same qualifications hold true to teach our children self-esteem and morals. You are certainly qualified for the job. Those young people's lives at Wade Hampton High are in your hands and God choose you for the job. What an awesome task.

E- Example – The teacher must be an example in life on and off the job. Your students are watching you. Stay strong and always abide in the Word of God. That is where your lesson plan is.

R – Refuge – A place of refuge is a place where one feels secure and safe. You are that place for many of your students and their parents.

R – Rescuer – This word is a person who rescues another from bondage or danger. What an honor it must be that God trusts you to be that person to so many people. He knew someone needed to be at WHHS to help those young people.

Y – Yield – Terry you are that person who have submitted, surrender and yield to God and because of that He has made you to be a teacher, an example, a refuge, and a rescuer. What a great person you are!

For the first letter, I think I did well. Lord, I know it's you that is helping me write these letters to my friends. I think this is a wonderful description of who Terry is to me and I can't wait until she reads it.

December 3, 2012

Since being diagnosed with cancer, I've thought about the phrase "in the meantime." What do you do in between the time that you ask and receive? For me, that's the time between when I was told on May 10, 2011, that I have Stage IV Colon Cancer and the time when the doctor will say, "I see no signs of the disease." Of course, in life, you will have a lot of those "in the meantime" periods. I know I have, and I'm still waiting for so many other prayers to be answered, like waiting for my children to be saved. But "in the meantime," I choose to bless the Lord with all my soul and all that is within me. I choose to continue to pray, pray and pray, and love, love and love. What are you waiting for and what are you doing while you wait?

Isn't that a question to answer?

December 4, 2012

Today I decided to answer the question: what do you do "in the meantime"? Many of us are living "in the meantime." In the meantime is not a wasted time. I have found in my life that it is a time of growth. It is a time "when the former page has been turned but the next page has not even been written yet." It is an attitude. It is a different way of thinking and a different way of acting. You choose to believe God at His word. While you wait, in the meantime, you hold on to the hope of glory. Who is that hope? Christ Jesus. You need to have confidence in Christ that what has been promised to you will come to pass. You need to stay connected to God through prayer daily so you can be strengthened and prepared for what will happen. We need to keep living and praying and hoping and believing no matter how long we have to wait. It's during this time that our faith is really tested and we must pass the test.

Joseph was 17 years old when he had a dream. Abraham was 90 when he was promised a son. What did they do in the meantime? God has left us examples to go by. In the meantime, while I wait for my complete healing, I will continue to bless the Lord with all my soul and all that is within me. I will continue to praise Him. I will continue to live for Him and love Him with all my heart. Jesus is my strength. I can't do anything without Him.

December 9, 2012

Yes, I have too much time to be thinking about things. So much is going on tonight. I am up tonight praying for my granddaughter and for a Pastor who is in the hospital. Gianna is at the hospital right now with a staph infection and they are putting an IV in her arm. I know she will be okay. Though Gianna is going through this, I know others are going through much more, so I won't complain. God is good even in the midst of our problems. He has all we need and that's why our eyes must stay on Him.

I went to Hallmark in Hampton to take a card to the owner on Saturday and there was a note that said "due to the death of," we are closed. I went there to take an encouragement card to the wife because she shared what her husband was going through. I wish I had gone sooner. I had her on my mind so much and kept putting off stopping by to talk and encourage her. I know I still can, but we need to do things when they are on our minds. Why wait?

Believe me; I'm not sad tonight because I realize that God is with all of us in our trials. He promised never to forsake us or leave us. I believe Him. I am so grateful tonight that He has allowed me to be here so I can share my feelings. God is a good God. He is wonderful. So tonight I am rejoicing, for this is the day that He has made!

I shared with my co-workers at LeCreuset something that was written just for me. It is the death of a matter and the birth of a new covenant, a new promise. God told me that I would live and declare the works of the Lord. The first part is done and now it's time for the second part. It's time now to declare His works. I am so glad I can close another chapter in my life and start a new one. It's time now to write about something else, and I am so looking forward to it in 2013—"A Better Me." I'm just going to endure like a good soldier. I want to live, so I will keep living while I'm living.

December 13, 2012

I'm excited today because I get to go to fellowship with my friends from LeCreuset. We are having our annual Christmas dinner at Elaine's house. It's so good to have friends that love you. I wanted to bless every one of them with a gift for Christmas. They all deserve it. Elaine loves to cook so I can't wait to see what she came up with. It's always good. I'm trying to decide what to wear. With my weight loss, it's hard to find something in my closet to wear. It's so funny because when I go to BiLo, people I know look at me hard to see if they recognize me. I say it's funny but it actually makes me want to cry. I know my weight loss makes me look different. I can look in the mirror and see that. Well, the good news is that I'm still here to look in the mirror. I know I will gain my weight back soon. It's only for a little while. My appetite is so much better than it was. My doctor told me not to be on any diet but eat whatever I want to. Well, here goes....

December 14, 2012

This is another day to rejoice. As I was looking at the pictures from last night with my friends from LeCreuset, I saw my face up close and thought to myself, "Who is that sad, skinny-faced woman?" I looked at the rest of the smiling women and could see the happiness in their faces, and I looked at my face and saw a sad-looking woman. Why do I look that way? What am I missing in my life? I was given life and I'm alive, so I should be rejoicing instead of worrying about my health. Help me, Lord to rest in you. You are so mighty good to me, God. I looked in the mirror this morning and said, "I'd rather be a skinny, alive woman than a fat, dead woman!" I'm alive and God is taking good care of me and my family. He has blessed us mightily. Forgive me for any doubts in my heart. I know, Lord, you are my healer and I know you want me to not die but live.

December 29, 2012

I am hearing in my spirit today to be fruitful and multiply. Let it be a blessing to the body of Christ. Others don't need to know who I am in Christ as long as I know who I am in Him. We not only had an awesome 2012, but 2013 will be more awesome than we could ever imagine. Psalm 92:12 says, "The righteous shall flourish like the palm tree: He shall grow like a cedar in Lebanon. Those who are planted in the house of the Lord shall flourish in the courts of our God. They shall still bear fruit in old age; they shall be fresh and flourishing to declare that the Lord is upright." I'm so glad that the righteous grow and flourish, not like grass, but like palm trees and cedars, which can withstand the harshest weather that comes. God's desire for us is that we live before Him and come to know Him as we study His word so that we will receive all that we need to be nourished to grow and to be fruitful.

Thank you, Lord, for allowing me to be fruitful so I can be a blessing to the body of Christ.

January 1, 2013

As this New Year comes in, I believe 2013 will be an amazing year. Those words were emailed to me by my friend, Peggy Parker. Amazing, meaning more than we will ever know. Though it seems that things have been hindered in my life and my ministry, I do know that what God has for me is just for me. If God is for me, no man can be against me. God, please forgive me of my sins and help me walk in Your Will. What is the Will of God for my life? That is the question. What is Your Will for my life in 2013?

Pastor Lewis said that this year the promises of God will be manifested in our lives. Lord, there has been so much said about your promises to me. Someone told me my life was like being a tree with branches extending out with much fruit and how it will be manifested in my life. God, you have been so amazing in my life already. You have done things that no one will ever know. You spared my life; you allowed me to live another year in spite of how things looked, in spite of what the doctors said or thought would happen to me; you made a way for us financial y in spite of what we had to pay for or do. Whatever we needed, it was there. You are our healer, our provider, our Father, and I thank you so very much for it. Last night, New Year's Eve, we had communion at midnight to bring in the New Year.

Since yesterday I have been thinking about my life and my desires. God, you know I need more of you. Help me learn how to study alone and give me more revelation of Your Word. Show me how to use my time more wisely.

Show me how to help others as you have sent others to help me. Show me what doors to go through; the doors I don't need to go through, please shut them and don't let me enter in. Help me to speak only life to myself and others. Lord, help me do only Your Will and not mine. Keep me out of your way. Help me and give me the wisdom to help others. Help me think more like you and love more like you. Save my sons and my family. I speak salvation upon their lives. God, help us be a blessing to the Kingdom of God. You know where you are taking us and the roads we must travel. Lead us safely and let the words that we speak be effective. That's what I would like you to do in this New Year. Amen.

January 8, 2013

Here it is, another season in my life. What is going to happen now? I'm waiting to get tested after my surgery. I'm not writing about my treatments much anymore because they are all the same. I hate each and every one of them, but am so thankful that they are working. My body has taken longer to heal from this surgery, but I am so very glad just to have made it. I look and feel 100% better. I am so very grateful to be among the living.

I was listening to TBN and a pastor was speaking about the year 2013 and the blessings to expect. He said that there are birth changes and new growth for the year 2013. I can't remember the pastor's name, but these are the things he predicted for 2013:

1. Increase your capacity to receive. There will be an abundance of more.
2. Enlarge your territory. There will be growth and expansion.
3. Re-adjust and realign your faith, your life.
4. God will silence and adversary. Prolonged battle will end.
5. Unusual and supernatural miracles will be demonstrated.
6. Financial anointing, constant anointing.
7. Total recovery and restoration. More than restored.

Those were great predictions, and I pray they will be manifested in my life in 2013.

January 9, 2013

Another day to give God thanks for all He has done. You are a mighty God, and I love you. Today I'm fasting for our pastors, for our church, for my family and for some special friends. God, help us be more than conquerors. We need to reach out to you more and more so that we can stay closer to you. It hurts me to think about all those who are hurting. I pray for my special friend, Lydia. God, please give her peace. She needs you right now. Let her know she is not alone and that you are right there beside her. So much is happening in this world, but we must remember that you have given us the power to be more than conquerors.

January 15, 2013

Jesus, we still don't understand who you are and who we are in you. As I read the book of John and see the life of Jesus and how the people, especially the Pharisees, did not believe who you were, my soul cries because there are people right now who don't believe. My soul cries because there have been times in my heart when I knew that God dwells in my heart, but the devil kept trying to lie to me and change my mind about who you are and who I am in Christ. We must stay focused on you continuously. We must not even blink because the enemy is trying to take our mind off you. The devil wants us to give up and not enjoy our lives. You said in Your Word, John 10:10 that you came "to give us life and more life abundantly." Let me live that abundant life.

January 22, 2013

Psalms 46:1-3 says, "God is our refuge and strength, a very present help in trouble. Therefore we will not fear, though the earth should change, though the mountains shake in the heart of the sea; though its waters roar and foam, though the mountains tremble with its tumult." No matter what is going on in our lives, we must remember that God is more than enough to handle all our problems, so today I am giving Him me! I needed to remind myself of this.

January 28, 2013

Tomorrow I will be doing a radio interview with an Internet radio station in New Jersey. It's called, "A Godly Woman's View," with Co-Pastor Anita Spaulding. My family and friends will be able to call in and be a witness to my testimony. I'm so excited to share my testimony with the world. I will also be having dinner with my friends from LeCreuset. I am so glad that God opened the door for me at LeCreuset. I worked with some wonderful people and now I can call them friends.

I have been reading my journals and, as I look back, I can see how far the Lord has brought me. "God is able to do exceedingly, abundantly; above all we can ever ask or think." God can bring us out of our misery. He certainly brought me out of mine. God is truly amazing, and He gets all the glory for the things He has done in my life. Healing belongs to Him. I am so glad for the opportunity to tell others about our God and that He is still in the healing business. There is none like Him. There were many days I asked God why I had to go through the things that I went through. None of it was easy, but it was necessary to go through the process. Without going through, I would not have this testimony. I would not have chosen this, but God knows how much we can bear when we don't. I never could have made it without Him.

January 29, 2013

I thank my friends for having dinner with me last night. I always look forward to having fun with my friends. I was thinking about friendship this morning and looked up the meaning of the word. It says to have a friend means that "no matter the difference that can exist between you and her, you can count on her when you need a shoulder to cry on, someone to laugh with, someone to celebrate with and cherish the sad and happy moments of your life journey." When I think about my friends, I can see the true meaning of friendship in each one of them. Each has her (or his) own purpose in my life. It's good to have friends that help you get through the hardest things in your life. Yes, I know God is the healer, but He has his earthly angels to help him out, too! I found a quote by Douglas Pagels which says, "A friend is one of the nicest things you can have, and one of the best things you can be." I find that to be true.

February 22, 2013

    It's Friday, and I'm not having a good day. I knew my insurance would be ending in June and I didn't want to wait until the last minute to get an extension. At least, I was hoping to get one. I read the paperwork that said if you are on disability while on COBRA, you can get a disability extension, so I sent Ms. Marsha an email asking her to help me with my COBRA extension. I called the insurance company and faxed them the information they requested. A representative called me back and told me today that I did not qualify for the disability extension because I did not report to them that I was disabled within the 60 days that is stated in the policy. She said that LeCreuset would have to approve me for the extension. I explained to her that I was out on disability when I signed up for COBRA, but she said because it doesn't state that I was, only that my employment was ending on December 31, 2011, I did not qualify for the extension. She said I had to go back to LeCreuset and get them to approve this decision. I can't believe this. My insurance ends on June 30th. What are we going to do now? Lord, please give me wisdom right now to know how to handle this. I don't qualify for anything. Where is all the help people say is out there? I am so glad I called about it today so I will have some time to get more information. Help me, Lord. Show me where to find help.

March 11, 2013

I couldn't sleep tonight. I was up reading the Web to see what was happening in the world. I came across this quote by Valerie Harper and thought it was great. "I'm not dying until I do." Wow! All of us will die, but we just keep living until we do! That blessed me tonight. I will continue to live while I'm living because I'm not dying until I do! I will have a CAT scan tomorrow at Charleston Cancer Center. I haven't had one since my surgery, and I am concerned about what they will see on my liver. I know the Lord is with me no matter what. I am praying that the doctor will say he doesn't see any sign of cancer. That will be great. Help me, Lord, to continue to put my trust in you.

March 12, 2013

I had an appointment for a CAT scan today at Charleston Cancer Center. I hate drinking that potion they give you before getting your test, and I was scared to hear what the doctor was going to say. After all I have been through, Lord, please let the cancer be gone. That was my prayer this morning. I found out later that I have to wait until my next appointment to find out the results. I hate waiting. I want to know now. This was so very hard. I can't believe we have to wait until the next visit. Well, I guess I need to reread what I wrote about waiting. I need to remind myself about learning how to wait. What can I do but wait? Lord, help me to keep positive thoughts.

You didn't bring me this far to leave me now.

March 15, 2013

I had an appointment with Dr. Steigler today. He set up my appointment for another guided paracentesis to be done on March 22nd at 9:00 a.m. Dr. Steigler always encourages me and now believes that I will not die but live. His nurse went over instructions for me not to eat or drink eight hours prior to the procedure. I had to go to the hospital for lab work and, also, to call to pre-register. I think I can remember to do all of this. I'm glad someone went with me to help me remember. My stomach is full with fluid again so I know I must do this. Help me, Lord. I can't do this without your help. I shared with Dr. Steigler that I had a CAT scan yesterday and am now waiting for the results. He just encouraged me to hold on to my faith. What else do I have but faith in God? He is my strength.

Isaiah 41:10 (NKJV)

"Fear not, for I am with you; be not dismayed, for I am your God. I will strengthen you, Yes, I will help you, I will uphold you with My righteous right hand."

March 16, 2013

Is it hard to keep believing? I was thinking about that while waiting for the results of my CAT scan. I have been sitting and thinking about my answer to this question. It's one that you have to put much thought into, especially if you have hard times in life. I wanted my answer to be honest and from my heart. I don't want my answer to be based on religion, but on my own experience. God already knows my answer so I want to be honest with you.

Is it hard to keep believing? How would you answer this question? Would you be ashamed if you answered yes? Would you be proud and answer no? What would make a person stop believing? Would sickness, divorce, financial problems, or loneliness make you stop believing? Are you going through problems and finding it hard to keep believing God's promises? I will be honest and say that there have been times in my life when it has been hard to keep believing, but that doesn't mean that I stopped believing in God; it just means I have doubts and questions that I can't answer.

Is it a sin to doubt? To me, the only time I will not have any doubts and have all the answers is when I arrive in Heaven. Right now I do have unanswered questions that are based on my circumstances. I have asked the question, "Why?" Is that doubt? We tend to be afraid to let others know that we have the "why" questions of life in our minds. We can't even ask "Why?" in church because we don't want others to think that we are not Christians. The church is the place we should be able to go to for help, but now it's the last place to turn to because of others judging you. I have found that unless you walk in another's shoes, wearing the exact same size and fit as the other person, you cannot possibly know what he or she is going through. There are no two cases alike in any circumstance.

So, is doubt a sin? Does God condemn us when we question Him? In times of doubt, go back to what you know is true. You know God is a healer, a provider, and a protector. We just know this, and we have to stand on it even if we don't see it. That's what faith is—believing without seeing. We will have times in our lives when we will walk in the valley, like David. When you are in the valley of doubt, just keep walking until you get out! Keep walking it out. Eventually, you will get to where God is leading you. I needed to write this for me. I need to keep walking it out. That's what my friend, Valerie Smalls, told me to do.....walk it out.

Psalm 33:20 *(NKJV)*

"Our soul waits for the Lord; He is our help and our shield."

March 21, 2013

I just received a knock at the door and it was FedEx with a box of beautiful lilies. Ms. Marsha and her sons made me smile and I needed to smile. ☺ Thanks so much for loving me and my family. I am truly blessed to have friends like you. My desire is to always make others smile and happy, and sometimes I don't know how to receive it for myself. I'm sitting here crying because I want to do so much to help them, and here they are, always doing for me. I'm so grateful for them. Ms. Marsha is one special lady and friend. This made my day!

March 22, 2013

Today I went to Colleton Medical Center for another guided paracentesis procedure to get fluidoff my stomach. The first time, they took eight liters of fluid from it; today they removed only four liters. The nurse told me that was a good sign that my liver was healing. That was good news. I pray I don't have to do this again. It's not the most pleasant procedure to have done. I cried the first time I went through it, but the nurses were so nice that they make the experience easier. The first time I had this done the nurse actually sent me a gift the next day at my house. It was a devotional called "Jesus Calling." I can't believe she did that. They really made me feel special today.

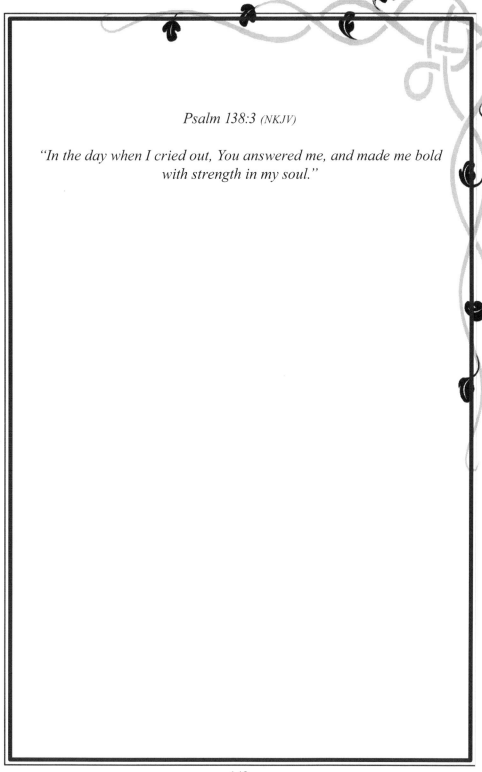

Psalm 138:3 (NKJV)

*"In the day when I cried out, You answered me, and made me bold
with strength in my soul."*

March 25, 2013
Spirit Week

Yesterday, Pastor Lewis reminded us of the Spirit Week we had in high school. How many remember that Spirit Week? It was a week of celebration. The purpose of Spirit Week was to get students excited about the big game on Friday night and to gain student support. During that week, students came together for a common goal of promoting the school team. They would decorate the halls with posters and banners. There was a different theme each day of the week, and students were encouraged to wear fun clothes that reflected each day's theme: Monday might be hat day; Tuesday, blue day; Wednesday, T-shirt day; Thursday, tacky day. On Friday, students would wear the school's colors and gather in the gym for a big pep rally, to meet the football team and cheerleaders, and to celebrate the big win that all anticipated that night.

Pastor Lewis did a great demonstration comparing Spirit Week with "This Week." He said that this is the week we should have Spirit Week, especially if we are among the "Redeemed." As he was bringing this to our attention, my mind went straight to my high school days over 30 years ago. Those were days we won't forget, but how many know that this week is a week we should never forget? How many of us remember what we are celebrating this week? So many of us forget about this glorious event that happened just for you and me! This is a week of celebrating our redemption. It's the week when Jesus suffered and died for us to live.

As we go through this week, we should not forget why we call this Friday "Good" Friday. The reason it is known as "Good" is that despite the terrible death of Jesus, the result of his pain, suffering, death, and resurrection was the opportunity for all of us who turn to God, through Jesus Christ, to be forgiven for our sins. That is a good thing! Romans 5:8 says "But God demonstrates his own love for us in this: while we were still sinners, Christ died for us." Isn't God GOOD?! As you go about your daily life this week, remember it was because of Jesus' death and resurrection that we can live, so let us celebrate this week by doing this:

Monday	Love……..be thankful
Tuesday	Love……..be thankful
Wednesday	Love……..be thankful
Thursday	Love……..be thankful
Friday	Love even more…..celebrate—this was the big day; because He died, we can live!
Saturday	Love more each day…..thank Him even more for the things He has done for us!
Sunday	Love and remember: "For God so loved the world that He gave His only begotten Son, that whosoever believes in Him shall not perish but have everlasting life." (John 3:16)

Now, that's love! He suffered and died for us. Then, early on Easter morning, He rose. Yes, Jesus is ALIVE. Because He lives, we can face tomorrow. This is how we can celebrate our "Spirit Week."

April 1, 2013

I woke up this morning quoting "Victory is mine saith the Lord." I believe it; victory is mine. God, you promised that I shall not die but live and declare the works of the Lord. I must believe the report of the Lord. I'm trying hard to be strong, knowing that my strength comes only from you. Now I know why that song and scripture came to me this morning. Today, April's Fool's Day, we received the results from my CAT scan and my blood work. It was hard waiting so long. I knew it wasn't good news. I felt it in my spirit. Dr. Holladay came in with his nurse, Nikki, to tell us the results of the scan, which showed that the cancer is back on my liver (yes, on the 30% that is left), and there are also several tumors on my lungs. We sat there and cried and cried. My husband cried along with me and the nurse. George held me close and told me it would be okay.

This is the conclusion of the report according to the radiologist: At the lung bases multiple small pulmonary nodules are now seen consistent with interval development of pulmonary metastasis. There is a new lesion within the liver consistent with a new liver metastasis; moderate amount of ascites [abnormal accumulation of fluid in open spaces between tissues and organs in the abdomen]. Wow, what can I say? After all I have been through—getting 70% of my liver removed; almost dying in the hospital; dealing with so much pain and fluid and other things that I can't even think of at this moment—the cancer is back. Lord that is not the news I wanted to hear.

Why, Lord? Why do I have to continue dealing with cancer? Of course, George was there with me, trying to comfort me. The doctor walked out to give us a moment. I told George it wasn't fair. I have served God with my life. Why do I have to go through so much pain? I hate chemo. I hate feeling nauseous day after day. I hate feeling so tired I don't want to get up in the morning. Why did I have to have 70% of my liver removed if the cancer was going to come back on the remaining 30%? I stayed in the hospital for 21 days and almost died just to hear from my doctor that the cancer is back. Lord, you have to help me with this. I don't understand. I just don't know what to do. My blood work was so much better. I still had a lot of fluid around my liver. I am still alive. God, you must have a purpose for my life. Please, God, help me understand your purpose. Help me, Lord. After giving us time to soak in the news, my doctor told me he would advise me to go back on chemo as soon as possible, but it was my choice. He told me again that my decision is quality of life versus quantity of life. Which would you choose? Lord, help me understand this.

April 10, 2013

I haven't written in my journal for days because I didn't know what to write. I'm not mad at God at all. How can I be mad at the only one who can help me? I am disappointed. I would be lying if I said I wasn't. This is a very hard pill to swallow. I can't even explain how I feel right now. God promised to work all things out for the good, so I'm just going to wait to see what He's going to do. I trust Him with my life. He will work this out. I know my diagnosis may sound bad, but His grace is sufficient. There is nothing too hard for God. I have to believe His promises even when things don't look good. God, I trust you. I give all of my cares to you. I can't handle any of them. I cast them at your feet. My faith will supersede my condition. Lord, all of my trust is in you.

April 13, 2013

Kingdom Touch Ministries did their first fund raiser for Relay for Life. It was very successful. I am very proud of my church supporting Relay for Life this year. Our theme was "Fun/Walk/Run." We did a four-mile walk for the cure. It was so good to see so many members participate, especially my pastors. They are always there for me and I really appreciate it. Of course, my husband was right there beside me cheering me on. The support from my family and friends really helps me keep fighting. Thanks, God, for blessing me with so many people who love me.

April 16, 2013

I made the decision to continue with the chemo, and we are back at the Cancer Center getting chemo in my veins. Yes, I'm back here at Charleston Cancer Center getting chemo. What other choice did I have? I have to continue to fight not only for myself but for my family and friends. I'm always telling others to keep fighting, so I know I have to. I know God will help me with each and every treatment. He promised. The wonderful thing is that my husband is right beside me, smiling like it's all good. We will be here until after 4:00 p.m.; then I get to take the other treatment home with me until Thursday. I read a story today about Michael Irvine and he used these words in his speech, "Look up, Get up, and Don't ever Give up!" Those words inspired me so much. I will be living by those words. I had to look up to God today for His strength, and get up to go for treatments, and I know I can't give up! Wow! I am writing while I'm waiting. Lord, help me to endure.

April 28, 2013

Today I woke up with this in my heart: Many people know His word, but if you are going to survive, you have to know His voice. Teach me your voice, Lord. Teach me how to respond to your voice. Teach me when to stand, when to speak, when to be silent, and when to cry out to you, God. Lord, I need you to teach me.

April 30, 2013

This was another day for chemo. I truly hate this, but I know it's part of my process to be healed. Lord, strengthen my mind today so I can receive this treatment. I will be hooked to my third treatment until Thursday. I can't wait until I'm disconnected. In the meantime, Lord, help me keep my mind on you. As I look around, I can see so many other people going through. All of us here are fighting for our lives. Sometimes I can't believe how I have made it. This fight with cancer has been one of the hardest things I have ever been through. Yes, cancer has taught me how to believe, how to love, and how to live. Even though I hate the hardship cancer has brought on my family, through it, I have learned lessons I know I would have never learned. Cancer has changed our lives, not for the worse, but for the better. That may sound crazy, especially considering how much I hate chemo, but the love I feel from God, from my family and from my friends is so different now. Cancer has taught me the power of love and it's great. Thank you, God, for all the times I have doubted you but you continued to give me peace.

Thanks for allowing me to rest in you during those hard times. Thanks for the gift of salvation.

May 2, 2013

I am so glad I get my pump removed today. This was a hard treatment. I had nausea for days and much fatigue. I wish I could have found something to help with the nausea. I am working on getting on George's insurance at his job at the end of June. Thank God they changed the rule about pre-existing conditions. I don't know what we would have done. I found out today that they will be sending me to another cancer center for treatment. They are sending me there because the other hospital offers more financial help for their patients. Thank God for that, but I hate to be leaving my nurses. They are so friendly here at Charleston Cancer Center. They know just how to help me by just looking at me. It's like they can read my mind. They know when the nausea is unbearable. I really will miss them. I don't have a choice though. We will need all the help we can get. My COBRA insurance was great paying my hospital bills even though we had our out-of-pocket expenses to pay. Lord, I thank you for sending help.

May 4, 2013

Today, George and I attended the Hampton County Relay for Life 8th annual Cancer Survivor Luncheon at Open Arms Fellowship in Hampton. There was a guest speaker as well as a great lunch. Due to limited seating, this event is held for Cancer Survivors Only. There were many people I knew who were there, many survivors, thank God. Each year they present an award for "Outstanding Survivor." I couldn't believe it when I heard my name. Now I know why Ms. Marsha asked if I was going; she knew about this. I cried like a baby. I can't believe I received "Hampton County Outstanding Survivor Award." What an honor that was. I felt really blessed.

Genesis 28:4 (NIV)

"I will bless them and the places surrounding my hill. I will send down showers in season; there will be showers of blessing."

May 8, 2013

This article, by Anthony Garzilli, with some minor editing for clarity, it appeared in the Jasper County Sun newspaper today :

" Relay for Life: 'We Can Still Survive' "
She's still here. She continues to live and speak at events, and when she opens the door each morning, she's thankful for another day to be able to see the sky. "I'm a living witness," Liz Orr said. Orr was diagnosed with Stage IV Colon Cancer in 2011.

She was given six months to live. She's had 21 chemotherapy treatments and two surgeries, had a fourth of her colon removed, and lost 70 percent of her liver. Orr's 38 years old. She has a 52-year-old husband, three sons, and last Friday night, at Jasper County's Relay for Life at Ridgeland Baptist Church, showed she still has a passion for living. "I'm still here," Orr said.

Born in Allendale, Orr lives in Hampton County, but is a member of Ridgeland's Kingdom Touch Ministries, and is a Jasper Relay for Life committee member.

Nancy Wellard, South Atlantic Division Community Manager for the American Cancer Society, and the committee were so impressed by Orr's enthusiasm, they honored Orr with the Mayor "Egg" Tuten award. Wellard met Orr last fall and realized "she was an incredible woman." Orr spoke at Hilton Head's Relay for Life and plans to speak at Hampton County's event.

She wants to spread the word that the American Cancer Society's efforts make a difference. "This is why we are doing this," Orr said. "After two years, I am surviving. It's because of all of your help. I'm still here." George Orr, Liz's husband, is her biggest supporter. The truck driver puts in long hours, but when he arrives home his focus is caring for his wife. "I've got to come out of my world and care about her and see what she needs," said George Orr, whose father died from lung cancer in 2007. "I thank God for this woman." It was a cool, rainy night last Friday, but 17 survivors, who have battled cancer for a combined 169 years, walked around the Luminaria- lined track.

Liz Orr, who played basketball when she was young, values each day. She has chemotherapy treatments every other week. So, between treatments, she travels, mostly to visit family. Recently, she went to watch her son, Anthony, play a spring football game at Johnson C. Smith University in Charlotte, N.C. Orr has surprised a cousin at his church. Orr, whose son, Randy, plays basketball in Japan, said the surgeries and treatments have been the toughest challenge.

But there she was Friday night, enthusiastically extolling the Relay for Life efforts. "I was diagnosed with Stage IV Colon Cancer; most of the time, that's it," she said. "But all of this is not in vain. I am still here. We can still survive. I'm going to be among the 90 percent (survivors). I'm going to be here next year. Your attitude has a lot to do with how long you live, and I refuse to die right now. I'm still here."

May 12, 2013

Here it is Mother's Day 2013. I'm so excited for the opportunity to bring forth God's Word at Huspah Baptist Church in Hampton this morning. I thank the Women's Ministry at Huspah for inviting me to speak again this year. I was honored to speak at their Mother's Day program last year too. I love Pastor Porter and his wife. They have been great supporters of me and my family along with their church family. I was nervous as usual but I kept telling God to enable me to do what He wants me to do. My husband always tells me I don't act nervous at all but it's because I allow Jesus to take total control and use me for His glory. He gives me the right words to say. I can do nothing without Him. My sons and the Orr family along with some friends came to support me. It was so good to look in the audience and see familiar faces. I wanted to do something special for all of the mothers so I bought red roses to give each of them. I thought about how we wait until someone dies before we give them flowers when they can't see them nor smell them.

The service was awesome. The same ladies who were on the program last year with me were there again this year with me. The mistress of ceremony was great and I love her sense of humor. The worship leader took us into a great worship experience. Church was so good. Afterwards we all went to Beaufort to dinner including George's cousin, Martha, who attended church with us. My sister-in-law Terry and her family met us in Beaufort for dinner. It was great food and fellowship. Everyone was so happy and then.......my husband got a devastating phone call. George's oldest sister Sandy was found in her apartment dead today. We had to stop the truck for a minute to digest the news. How could this be? I just spoke to her last week. She was so excited about buying Mother's Day gifts for her church. What a sad day this turned out to be. My sister-in-law Sandy at the age of 52 is dead. Lord how much more can we endure......

Sandy Orr
Sister-in-law

May 14, 2013

Here it is, another day at Charleston Cancer Center; another day of chemo. Thank you, God, for life. Today I will not complain. Please, Lord, strengthen me through this treatment. My hemoglobin was low today—10.7; my red blood cells were also low—3.55. I will be more mindful of my diet and eat the right things to build my blood back up. Give me wisdom, Lord. Today I was thinking about what I want people to see in me as I go through my journey. I really want others to see that there is life with cancer and after cancer. I want others to see my faith in Christ Jesus. I want to inspire others, so, Lord, help me be stronger.

May 15, 2013

Yesterday, while I was at the Charleston Cancer Center, I was writing about wanting to inspire others. While I was sitting there, I started getting weak and dizzy. I called the nurse and she took me to the private room. I began shaking and having chills. The nurse called my doctor and he told her to call the ambulance. I couldn't believe how fast things can happen. I was sitting there getting my chemo when, all of a sudden, I began feeling bad and shaking. I called Debbie Brown and Tish, the ladies, who had brought me to the Center, to let them know I had to go to the hospital. They came right away and accompanied me. They called George to let him know they were taking me to Trident Hospital.

Apparently, I had an allergic reaction to one of my chemo drugs. I had to stay one night at Trident, and Dr. Holladay released me the next day. That was so crazy. You can be doing well one minute and then, the next thing you know, you are being carried away in an ambulance. I am so grateful, God. I just prayed and prayed and asked God to guide the doctor's hand. Thank you, Lord, for healing my body.

June 22, 2013

Yesterday I shared a special prayer with my co-workers at LeCreuset. Yes, I still call them co-workers because they still treat me like one. This is what I shared with them:

Good morning, my family & friends, I woke up this morning feeling the blessings of the Lord and thanking Him for all He has done for me. I thought about how God has blessed me with so many wonderful people in my life such as all of you. I wanted to share this prayer I found on the Internet with you this morning to help you through the day. I pray each of you has a glorious day!

Workplace Prayer:

My Heavenly Father, as I enter this workplace, I bring your presence with me. I speak your peace, your grace, your mercy, and your perfect order in this office. I acknowledge your power over all that will be spoken, thought, decided, and done within these walls.

Lord, I thank you for the gifts you have blessed me with. I commit to using them responsibly in your honor. Give me a fresh supply of strength to do my job. Anoint my projects, ideas, and energy so that even my smallest accomplishment may bring you glory.

Lord, when I am confused, guide me. When I am burned out, infuse me with the light of the Holy Spirit. May the work that I do and the way I do it bring faith, joy, and a smile to all that I come in contact with today. Amen.

I pray that each of you will receive that prayer in your spirit. I love all of you and miss you very much.

July 1, 2013

Can you believe that I cannot receive chemo because my deductible and out-of-pocket maximum with my new insurance have to be met first? I have to wait until I have met my deductible and my $6,500.00 out-of- pocket maximum before they will start my chemo. Wow, they don't care that I could die without it! Here I am in need again. I had to go on my husband's insurance at Robert Elliott Trucking. Thank God they have insurance or I don't know what we would have done. I'm grateful for Cynthia Long, who helped me complete the paperwork in time. My COBRA insurance ended on June 30th and I received the new insurance on July 1st. I didn't realize the out-of-pocket maximum and deductible were so much.

I'm waiting to see if we can get payments set up. I filled out the financial paperwork for St. Francis Hospital. The lady I met with was very nice and very helpful. I explained what we were going through and told her we were not able to get any help. She looked at my paperwork and said, "You are now." I cried right then and there. My issue now is still the $6,500.00, but she said they can help with that, too. I know God will supply all our needs. Nothing is impossible with Him. He always has a ram in the bush.

July 23, 2013

We are at Roper/St. Francis Cancer Center. It is a very nice place. I was very nervous coming here, but I know it will be even better than before. I will be taking these treatments until December. We are praying that I will have no side effects. George is by my side, smiling, as always. I will miss the nurses at Charleston Cancer Center but I will continue to see them when I come see Dr. Holladay and my favorite nurse, Nikki. They were so compassionate and kind there. I'm looking at the nurses here and I see no smiles, at least not yet. I'm sure that once they get to know me and I get to know them, things will be fine. Lord, why do I have to go through so many changes? I know I will make it.

I am so grateful for my brother, Tony, and my pastors at Kingdom Touch Ministries. They are always there for us. I know they love me; they show it with their unwavering support. Yes, the Lord supplied all we needed, and now I'm here starting another round of chemo at a new cancer center. The place is very beautiful. I have my own space and television. That is something new. I think I will be all right. Thanks, Lord, for giving us all we need.

August 26, 2013

Today, I went to Peggy Parker's house to plan my birthday party and meet the caterer with my friends Coretta Orr, Annette Mole and Annette Griffin. It was so good to get out. When we got there, Peggy had refreshments for us. When the caterer arrived, I found out that he was a manager at LeCreuset in Bluffton. I was so excited. His name is Geist, and he was so funny. He told me he heard my name so much from other employees at LeCreuset. It was as if I knew him already. He had some great ideas about the menu for the party. I just let my friends decide on what to have. I can't believe how blessed I am to have wonderful people in my life who would go to the limit for me. I feel truly blessed right now. Afterwards, Peggy took us to a great seafood restaurant. The food was delicious, as I knew it would be. We had a great time. It was a great day. Thanks, God.

September 2, 2013

I am home from my vacation. George, Jamel, Randy and their friends drove me to visit with my brother, Tony, in Virginia for the Labor Day weekend. Anthony couldn't come with us because of his football game. We left on Friday afternoon and came back about midnight on Sunday. While we were at my brother's house we went to Virginia's beach on Saturday. That was so exciting. I haven't been to the beach in almost 20 years. It was amazing seeing how beautiful the beach is. God created a wonderful place for us to live. The sun, the waves, and the water were refreshing. The people were really enjoying what God has given us. We walked down the beach with our shoes off. It felt so good to have the sand between my toes. I wanted to cry. I am still alive to enjoy God's wonderful beach. We stopped in Lumberton, North Carolina, to visit with George's sister, Jackie, on the way back, and she and her husband prepared dinner for us. We had oxtails, curried chicken, jerk chicken, and beans and rice. My brother-in-law can cook that Jamaican food! I am so happy. I am still enduring chemo, but the good news is that I am still alive to enjoy my family.

September 4, 2013

Today I was sitting at Roper/St. Francis Cancer Center getting my 34th chemo treatment and looking around at the glory of God. Everyone here is fighting for his or her life. It takes this to see how precious life can be. We need to stop complaining about how our life is and start celebrating each and every day for what it is: our present, our gift, given by God to enjoy. This is the day the Lord has made, and I will rejoice and be glad in it in spite of my circumstances. It's almost midnight, it is midnight, and I can't sleep. I am still rejoicing. My husband is sleeping like a baby and looks so peaceful. LOL....He's a big teddy bear.....I pray that I can go to sleep and have a peaceful night. I do know when I get up in the morning I will tell God thank you! I think I will do it right now.....

September 8, 2013

I woke up this morning tired and nauseous as usual after a treatment. As I was walking back from the kitchen, I looked down at the floor and saw blood. I panicked like crazy. I looked at my body to see where I was bleeding. I looked down and saw that the line hooked to my port was hanging on the floor and blood was coming out of it. I didn't know what to do. I called the home infusing company that furnishes the pump and chemo to ask what I needed to do. The nurse tried to calm me down so I could clean and flush the line and re-access my port. I told her I couldn't do it. I was so nervous. She then told me to go to the emergency room at the hospital. Oh, my God. I was so scared.

I called my neighbor, Coretta, who came quickly to my house to take me to the hospital. I called George, who wanted to come home right then and there, but he was too far away. I told him I would call him when we got to the hospital. Once at the hospital, the nurse took me back to a room and cleaned and flushed my line to re- access the port. There was nothing to it, but the blood and the fact that the chemo was getting on my floor really scared me. Lord, please help me. I guess I slept badly last night and the line was loosened. I will make sure the nurses put tape around it next time. I'm glad everything worked out okay and now I am home safely, continuing with my chemo. I can't wait until tomorrow when this pump comes off.

September 9, 2013

When you think what you are going through is so bad, you need to pray that God will allow someone to come along and share his or her testimony with you, and then you will see how incredibly blessed you really are, and will never allow self-pity to come into your life. My husband and I shared a meal with Barry Brunson and his lovely wife tonight, and we were able to share our testimonies with each other. I can see why the Bible tells us that, "They overcome him with the word of their testimony." It was an amazing time, and we were all able to encourage one another. Not only are Barry and I going through it, but our spouses are going through just as much, so please also pray for the caregivers as well as the patient. We are truly blessed, and God has allowed us to live to share the goodness of the Lord.

Barry purchased us T-shirts that say, "Thank God for allowing this day." Please, let us thank God as we celebrate our lives and others who are going through with cancer. We are survivors determined to not die but live and declare the works of the Lord! Join us and "thank God for allowing this day!" Barry and I are both dealing with Stage IV Cancer, but we are determined to (in the words of Valerie Harper) "not die until we do"—when God says so. Barry is a three-year survivor and I am a two-year survivor with many more years to look forward to.

October 7, 2013

    I am excited because my nurse called to tell me that they are cancelling my treatment this week so I can have a mental break. I need it so very much, and I can now feel my best for my party! I'm so happy about it......... even just little things make me happy. ☺

October 11, 2013

What a wonderful day this was, a day of joy, happiness, peace and many blessings. I don't know what I have done to deserve such favor from the Lord. I thank Peggy Parker, Annette Mole, Annette Griffin, Coretta Orr, Gloria Fields, Linda Harris, Crystal Lewis, Jill Knight, Sally Hiers, and so many others who blessed me with this party. My brother came in on Thursday night with his family, Ro and Dee Dee, to be here for my birthday. Friday morning was great. We had breakfast from Reid's deli, then got dressed and went to Bluffton to take my sisters, Gloria and Linda, to Peggy's house. After leaving there, we took my sister-in-law, Ro, to Walterboro to Belk's. I'm so glad Tony was here because he drove us everywhere. We got home at 4:30 p.m. with enough time to get dressed and go to the party. I'm glad I went to get the dress from Cato's on Thursday with Valerie Smalls. She took me to get my nails done, too. What a blessing. Lydia came to the house to ride with us to the party. I was late, as always. I couldn't wait until everyone got dressed so we could leave.

My friends gave me a 49th birthday party. I told them that this year I wanted to have a "Celebrating Life" birthday party. I have wonderful friends. My friends wouldn't let me do anything for the party. On trips to Charleston for chemo, Debbie Brown and Tish took me to buy plates, cups, and forks from Costco. Ms. Marsha even took me shopping for my party, and I can't forget Annette Mole taking me to Bluffton to shop for something to wear. Even my Co-Pastor from Kingdom Touch Ministries gave me money for supplies. All I had to do for my party was buy something nice to wear. Debbie and Tish even took care of the things I needed for the bar—non-alcoholic, of course. I was blessed beyond measure. I can't forget the fact that the party was at Peggy Parker's house. Her house, which is on Myrtle Island in Bluffton, is so beautiful! Annette Griffin hired a photographer so I will have wonderful pictures to remember the party by. My friends thought of everything! I can't forget about my Chef, Geist, who cooked the most wonderful meal we could have had. The food was delicious. He cooked just for me.

I wish Randy could have been there. He is overseas playing

basketball and couldn't get there for the party. Anthony couldn't come either because of his football schedule. Jamel was there with Kendra. George looked really good and my dress with the accessories came out great! I felt beautiful. I felt so incredibly happy. It's a blessing to have friends and family like this. They showed so much love. When we arrived, I couldn't wait to get out of the car. I felt like a movie star. Annette Griffin was greeting the guests and the photographer and his sister were taking pictures. They took lots of pictures of me and my guests as we walked up the walkway. I had to wait on George because he was greeting people getting out of their cars. When we finally walked to the back of the house, all I could do was cry. It was breathtaking. It was absolutely beautiful. The tables, the lights, the yard, the big tent....it was as if it was a dream. I could not have asked for anything more beautiful. Even the weather was perfect and the moon shined so brightly above us. The lights on the trees were magical. God, you are so amazing! What did I do to deserve this?

Some of the guests were already there and others kept coming in all night. I must say I did not think so many would come, since we had the party in Bluffton, but it was like they were looking forward to it. Many of them called us to get directions. Even our State Representative, Bill Bowers, came to show support. I really appreciated that. He is our friend. Peggy was a wonderful hostess, along with Jill and Sally. They know how to host a party! Peggy had her jazz band there playing music. As I said before, they thought of everything.

My nephew, Dewayne, came with his family, and his father-in-law came with them. Of course, my family from LeCreuset came. Mrs. Faye came in from the airport to be there. My Orr family was there supporting me, as always. Even Aunt Margaret came. I was so glad to see her. She promised me that she would be there and she did come. My sister, Gwen, and her husband, Robbie, came from Allendale. Wow, I couldn't believe that! What really surprised me was a friend I had never met before came from Savannah. We have talked and prayed together for a year now on the phone, and she surprised me by coming to my party. I never thought I would see her there. I sent the invitation but never thought she would show up. I can't list all the people from Hampton who came; the list would be too long. I do remember that Betty and Ronnie Mixson arrived at the same time we did.

This day I will never forget—the day that God showed me just how much my friends and family really love me! Someone asked me why I didn't wait to have a special party for my 50th birthday next year. I told the person that every birthday is special, and we should never wait for a particular birthday, but celebrate each one that God blesses us with. I will worry about my 50th birthday next year, but what could I possibly do to top this one? I thank everyone for their love and support. So many people supported me, and I am truly grateful. My heart is so full right now.

November 15, 2013

Last week I completed 40 rounds of chemo. Everything I have heard about chemotherapy is true. I always wondered why doctors wanted people to take this medicine if it makes them so sick. I would not have known the answer to this question if I had not gone through it. I now know why people take it. It's rather simple. Because you want to live, you will take anything that gives you hope for life. Yes, you tolerate it because you want to live. The chemo may make you sick, cause you to be so tired and fatigued that you can hardly walk at times, kill your appetite, make you nauseated day and night, cause you to hurt all over your body, but it is worth it when you know that it is helping keep you alive. This is the process that God has chosen to heal my body, so I have to have the faith to trust God with my life. I have learned to rest when I feel bad, and get up and do when I feel better. You just keep going even when you have those bad days. Those bad days and feelings are a part of the process. I have learned to just walk through, knowing that tomorrow will be better.

I am so blessed and humbled by what I have learned. My life is more wonderful than before. I have gained so much more living with cancer than living without it, and I am so grateful. This may sound crazy to many, but it makes a lot of sense to me. God has a purpose and a plan for our lives. He is always at work making us more like His Son. He can work all things out for our good.

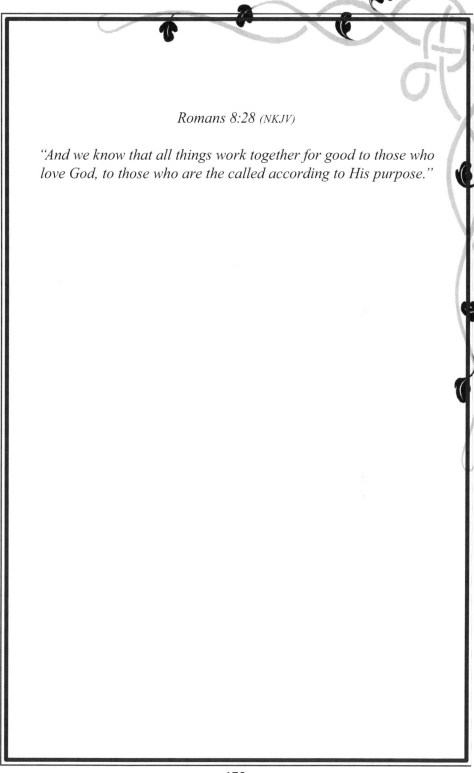

Romans 8:28 *(NKJV)*

"And we know that all things work together for good to those who love God, to those who are the called according to His purpose."

November 16, 2013

Today the most amazing thing happened. My sister-in-law, Terry, came and took me out to brunch at Shoney's in Walterboro. I should have known it was all a plot to get me out of the house. When we arrived back at my house, I walked in and there were women there dressed like angels saying to me, "We are your angels; come on in." Wow, talk about a surprise! My friends, Annette Mole and Marshal Colleton, were there, too. The angels came from Raleigh, North Carolina, to decorate my house for Christmas. Can you believe that? They were a Colon Cancer awareness group who came down just to decorate my house for Christmas, and it was decorated beautifully. There were angels all around my house; everywhere I looked there were angels! My Christmas tree was amazing. I would never decorate a tree like that. My fireplace was gorgeous with big bows and more angels. Lord, what did I do to receive this wonderful gift? I found out my son, Randy, had met with the angels from Raleigh and told them my story. He even took pictures of my house for them so they could choose the right color scheme for the decorations. God is so wonderful.

What wonderful ladies, as well as a male angel, I met that day. The male angels' name was Trey. He was so sweet. I love my Trey. We spent time together sharing our stories, and we sat and cried together. Most of them were affected by Colon Cancer in one way or another. Mrs. Carol Peeples started this foundation in memory of her mother, who died from Colon Cancer. I can't believe they came all the way to South Carolina just to make me happy! The good part was that they will also come back in January to take down all of the decorations. Now, that's great! What a blessing I received on this day. My husband also was a part of the planning of this great day. I should have known something was going on that day. What a great surprise! Thanks to Mrs. Carol and the Angels for blessing me.

November 30, 2013

We had a wonderful Thanksgiving Holiday. I really enjoyed my family. I'm so thankful to have such wonderful family and friends in my life. Now that Thanksgiving is over, our minds shift directly to Christmas. Even before Thanksgiving was over many of us were thinking about Christmas. Well, I have a question. If you could have any gift you wanted for Christmas, what would you ask for? Think about that for a moment. What would your answer be? I know what I would ask for.....complete healing.....no more chemo.

I found this wonderful prayer for Christmas: "Father, give us eyes to see the baby Jesus in a new and fresh way this Christmas season. Help us to see him as he really is–a king sleeping in a stable. Give us ears to hear the angels singing. Give us feet like the shepherds to go swiftly to Bethlehem. Give us hands like the Wise Men to offer him the best that we have. Give us hearts of love to worship him. Amen."

December 2, 2013

A friend of mine, Joyce Hallenbeck who helped me edit this book, sent me a wonderful poem I would love to remember for the New Year. I shared it with my co-workers at LeCreuset and my other email buddies. Now I have a Christmas prayer and a New Year's prayer.

A Prayer for the New Year

Thank you, Lord, for giving me
The brand New Year ahead.
Help me live the way I should
As each new day I tread.

Give me gentle wisdom
That I might help a friend.
Give me strength and courage
So a shoulder I might lend.

The year ahead is empty.
Help me fill it with good things
Each new day filled with joy
And the happiness it brings.

Please give the leaders of our world
A courage born of peace
That they might lead us gently
And all the fighting cease

Please give to all upon this earth
A heart that's filled with love,
A gentle, happy way to live
With your blessings from above.

The New Year lies before you
Like a spotless tract of snow.
Be careful how you tread on it,
For every mark will show.........
- Charlotte Anselms -

That was just what I needed to start a new year. Thanks, Joyce. You have been a blessing in my life.

December 20, 2013

I was thinking about how I could celebrate Jesus' birthday. So many times we have said that Christmas is just another day. Well, it's not just another day, but a day set aside to celebrate our God's, our King's, birthday. He may not have been born on this day, but it's the day we set aside to celebrate His wonderful birth. Our Father looked down on us and sent His only son to redeem us, and I'm so glad about it. We must not treat Christmas as just another day. It's much more than that. We should do something special for someone else. As we celebrate the birth of our great God, we need to remember those who are less fortunate than we are. All we have to do is just look around; I'm sure we'll find someone. We need to spend time with our family and friends, and love on them. Let's not take another Christmas for granted, for on this day "A child was born," our Lord and Savior, Jesus Christ. I needed to remind myself of this.

December 31, 2013

Lord, I have asked so much of you. Please forgive me for every doubt that I have shown in my life. Lord, for the end of the year, my prayer now is that you take this cup away from me. Nevertheless, let Your Will be done, not mine. Help me to know my purpose and walk in it. Use me for your glory. Use my condition for your glory. I pray that every word in this journal can help others go through theirs. I thank you forever.

The Journey Continues...
but the Story Ends

The journey continues, but my story will end here for now. Only by the grace and strength of God am I able to make this journey. No one wants to hear the words, "you have cancer." I cried. I knew my life would forever change. This journal covers two years, seven months of my emotions, my thoughts, my therapy following my initial diagnosis of Stage IV Colon Cancer. I had to write my emotions down because I was embarrassed to share them with others at the time. I didn't want my family and friends to know what I was really feeling. There were days when my faith reached its breaking point. During those times, I found out that is when God's grace will carry you through the most. His grace is sufficient.

God always had angels of love surrounding me everywhere I went. The earthly angels were there at every cancer center and every hospital and every doctor's office. The nurses at Charleston Cancer Center, at Roper/St. Francis Cancer Center and Trident Cancer Center were God's angels who have shown me so much love and kindness and compassion. God has truly blessed me with the best support team anyone could have, including my oncologist, Dr. Charles Holladay; my surgeon Dr. Karl Steigler; and my primary care doctor, Dr, Neal Shealy. I can't forget the nurses at Coastal Carolina in Walterboro, at The Healthcare Center in Hampton, and my great home health nurse, Mrs. Jill Knight from the State Department of Health. I have to mention the best nurse a doctor can have which is Ms. Nikki at Charleston Cancer Center. She has been so good to me. This journey has enabled me to meet so many people and helped me develop so many friendships. I wish I could name every single one, but I know I would miss someone.

My husband—my best friend, my soul mate—has been there for me every step of the way. I can't say enough about him. He has shown me what it really means to love someone. I love him so much. He has shown what the wedding vows are all about. Through sickness and health, George has been right there beside me. My sons, Jamel, Randy and Anthony, are the best sons anyone could have. They have shown so much love and support. All three of my sons call me almost every day to check on me. I am so grateful for my two grandchildren, Jalen and

Gianna, who make me smile whenever I talk to them or see them. And I have to mention my adoptive granddaughters, Samaria and Zoe. I am blessed to have a wonderful family, including my big brother, Tony, and his wife, Ro; my sisters, Linda and Gloria, who took care of me when I came home from the hospital; and my surrogate mother, Mrs. Lizzie Priester, who never forgets to send me a birthday card or holiday card. I can't forget Mrs. Paula Cope who sends me a card almost every week.

To my brother-in-law, Tim, and sisters-in-law, Terry, Jackie, Georgia and Sandy, who were there supporting and loving us, thank you dearly. Thanks to Coretta Orr, Barbara Boles, and the rest of my Orr family, who fed me and drove me to Charleston numerous times for my treatments. To my family at LeCreuset, what can I say about you? You are all earthly angels to me.

I had the best bosses in the world at LeCreuset, Elaine, Archie and Mrs. Faye Gooding. Thanks for all of you at LeCreuset, my friends who have helped us so very much in every way. Ms. Marsha, you are forever in my heart. Thanks for being a friend.

When I was told I had cancer my heart almost stopped. Time stopped. For a second, I didn't feel a thing. The doctor put me back to sleep, but when I woke up the next day; I knew my life would be changed forever. It was difficult to hear those words, but I knew I could not have a pity party; I just had to believe in God's Word like never before. From the day I gave my life to Christ, I have read His Word and loved every word I read. I began to soak in everything I read, especially the Old Testament. I loved reading about Moses, and David, and Psalms, and Proverbs. What I loved most was how David was called a man after God's own heart, especially with his background. After studying David's life, I wanted to be a woman after God's own heart. I knew that, though I was not perfect, I could be a woman after God's own heart. I am so glad that I began to seek God like never before.

The day after he diagnosed me with cancer, I told my doctor that I was not going to die. Not yet. The doctor walked to the door, turned around, and said that, for some reason, he believed my case would be different. Now, when I visit my surgeon he smiles with me and believes Proverbs 18:14, which says, "The spirit of a man will sustain him in sickness." A person's attitude, a person's faith, will help him recover from sickness. I will continue to trust God with all my heart. I have no one else to trust.

When your doctor tells you that you have cancer, your mind immediately begins to think about only one thing… death. Unfortunately, that's the first thought that came to my mind, but my second thought went straight to Jesus. I thought about what He would say and what He would do. Lord, you promised me so many things in my life and they haven't happened yet, so I know it's not time for me to die. When you have been diagnosed with cancer, so many negative thoughts come to your mind. You begin thinking about when death is going to happen and what things need to be done before you die. Yes, I did begin getting ready to die at the time of my diagnosis. Though I trusted God with all my heart, I still got ready to die, until one day God reminded me that I was telling others that "I shall not die but live," but my actions were preparing myself to die. I would think about dying during particularly difficult times dealing with the cancer, or when I heard about others who were diagnosed after me but had already died. When I had those thoughts, I was able to push them away and speak the Word over my life. I am so glad for the Word of God!

I have been so blessed to have my pastors and other pastors from South Carolina, Georgia, Texas, New York, New Jersey (Bishop & Pastor Samuels), North Carolina (Pastors Erol & Jackie Tinling), and other states praying for us. When I was at my lowest point, Jesus always had someone there to call or come by to pray for me. I am so grateful for all those people who prayed for me and my family.

The list would be too long if I mentioned everyone by name. I pray you know who you are. I do know that all of Hampton County has supported us so much. We have received so many cards, donations, food, prayers and encouragement. We live in a wonderful county and a great community. Thanks for people like Mary Ann Rivers, who, when she heard about my diagnosis, came and ministered to me about her experience with Stage IV cancer to show me that I, too, could make it through this. After all, she is a living witness.

We have great neighbors, like Mrs. Lucille Kinard who has shared her garden with us and fed us so many good meals. Every church in Hampton and the surrounding area has had me on their prayer lists. I want to especially thank my church family at Kingdom Touch Ministries, who have spoiled me with so much love. I have to thank my

Sister2Sister group that has loved me through all of this, Sabrina, Valerie, Lydia, Sonya. There are so many people - family, and friends like Peggy Parker — who have been sources of encouragement and love, and I just want to say thank you, although thank you is not enough to express our gratefulness for all of you. I do know that your faith, family and friends will get you through this.

I thank God for His healing power. I thank God for being with me and giving me peace. When David says, in Psalms 23:4, "Though I walk through the valley of the shadow of death, I will fear no evil," this lets me know that I will have to walk through the valley but not stay in it.

I thank God for that. I know that God has allowed me to live because He has a purpose for me. It is only because of His grace and mercy I am still here. I know my purpose is to help others in their journey fighting cancer. I know it's to inspire others and let them know to never give up. My prayer has been, "Lord, never let me look like what I'm going through." God has answered that prayer for me. Many have told me that if I didn't share my testimony with them, they would have never known I was dealing with cancer. Even my nurses said to me that I didn't look like I was a cancer patient. All I know is that if it had not been for the Lord, I would not be here. My prayer is that I can do the Will of my Father. My life belongs to Him and I give Him all the glory.

I have kept this journal for myself, but I decided to share it with some friends, who suggested that I write it in book form and get it published so that it could help others who are going through. They suggested that I share my testimony with others on how I coped with cancer. As I reread what I have written, the words inspire me, and I can see the hand of God in all I have gone through and am still going through, so I had to share it with others. I would love to have a great ending to let you know that God has totally healed my body and I no longer live with cancer, but I don't have that testimony yet. I believe it is soon to come. I am still in my waiting time. I want others to know that there is life during cancer.

Yes, I do mean life during cancer because I am still dealing with the disease. Nevertheless, I am encouraged and try to live each day to its fullest. Every Sunday I am in church at Kingdom Touch Ministries in Ridgeland. If I'm not there, I'm on vacation or at another church. I know how much I need God's Word. I live on God's Word. My life depends on God's Word. I have to hold on to my faith, and faith comes by hearing the Word of God. I'm blessed to be able to say that my husband is right there with me each Sunday praising God. What a time we have praising God in spite of our circumstances! This experience with cancer has certainly brought my husband and me closer together, and I'm so glad.

My life now is more precious than before. I see more joy even in the small things of life. My time now is more precious. I prioritize my time now. I spend more time with the important things in life—my God, my family, my friends. My life has been redefined. I'm not sure how many more chemo treatments I will need. All I know is that Jesus promised to be right there with me.

What advice would I give someone facing cancer? It is to trust Jesus with your life and believe in the Word of God; hold on to your faith and remember to take one day at a time, because that is our gift, the present. Life goes on, and we must live it and be glad in it. Live each day like it's your last day, live life to the fullest each day. Enjoy the sunshine and the rain. Be grateful for all things. Each day now, I look outside and thank God for the natural beauty that He has given us like the sun, the moon, the stars, the flowers, the trees.

My other advice is to watch your body for changes and do something about it right away. Go to your doctor and have regular checkups. Our bodies will let us know when something is wrong if we just pay attention to them. Did I have warning signs? Yes, but I ignored them. I was too busy to see a doctor. I was hoping the pain would just go away. I am so grateful now for gallstones. I probably wouldn't be here today if I hadn't had surgery to remove my gallbladder. That's how my cancer was found. I am grateful to God for allowing the doctor to see the cancer on my liver. What's weird is that I had had a colonoscopy about eight weeks before the gallbladder surgery and the cancer was not found on the colon at that time! I know it was God who led me back to the doctor to let him know that something else had to be going on in my body. The pain was now radiating from my stomach to my back. I am glad I finally listened to my body.

I am doing well now thanks to our savior, Jesus Christ. He is always with me. He is forever faithful. God has truly blessed me and because of Him, I am still here! Be Blessed!

Conclusion

March is Colon Cancer Awareness month. The disease is the second leading cause of cancer-related deaths for U.S. men and women combined. Recent statistics estimate that 142,000 new cases will be diagnosed this year, with the disease claiming more than 50,000 American lives each year. Colon Cancer often has no symptoms at all until it is at an advanced stage. You can reduce your risk of developing the disease through regular screening. Beginning at age 50, everyone should be screened for Colon Cancer.

A cancer diagnosis can turn your world upside down. You may not know what to do for your physical health, and you'll also have to deal with the many confusing emotions you are feeling. And then there are worries about your physical appearance and about whether the treatment may affect how you look. And, no doubt, you'll also wonder how you can stay positive and hopeful through the treatment process.

For someone living with cancer, the support of family and friends is critical in their journey. According to the National Cancer Institute, having family and friends available for support has a positive effect on how patients adjust to their diagnosis and treatment.

Cancer is So Limited
It cannot cripple Love
It cannot shatter Hope
It cannot diminish Faith
It cannot destroy Peace
It cannot kill Friendship
It cannot suppress Memories
It cannot silence Courage
It cannot invade the Soul
It cannot steal Eternal Life
It cannot conquer the Spirit
It cannot lessen the Resurrection
-author unknown-

"But those who hope in the Lord will renew their strength. They will mount up on wings like eagles. They will run and not be weary. They will walk and not faint." (Isaiah 40:31)

Liz
Your Fight For Life

Amazes me –
> *and even:*
> *Hushes the mouths of some,*
> *Encourages the weak,*
> *And increases praise to the Almighty One!*

I tell you
Your Fight For Life

Shows me what God can do –
> *and even:*
> *Breaks shackles off the bound,*
> *Builds the faith of the weary,*
> *And shuts the mouth of the enemy!*

Your Fight For Life

- Jackie Tinling

Oh Give Thanks...............

Psalm 106:1-2 says, "Praise the LORD! Oh, give thanks to the LORD, for He is good! For His mercy endures forever. Who can utter the mighty acts of the LORD? Who can declare all His praise?"

I want to give thanks to God for if it wasn't for Him and His unending love and grace, I don't know where I would be right now. I want to thank my loving husband, George, and my children and grandchildren, who have stood by my side and loved me more than I could have imagined. I also want to give thanks to all the wonderful people who have been praying and supporting me and my family. I feel so incredibly blessed to live in a communitywhere people love one another. I want to thank all the churches who had me on their prayer lists. The Word of God teaches us in James 5, "The effectual fervent prayer of a righteous man availeth much." So I thank God for your prayers and support.

When you are going through your trials know that God is there with His arms open wide to comfort you and to hold you. Only God is able to help us go through and help us to endure. We can't depend on our own strength and we need to know that God doesn't require us to be strong for His strength is made perfect in our weakness. I found out God doesn't give us what we can handle but He helps us handle what we are given.

My trials have made me so thankful for life. I have slowed down and now am enjoying my life, my family and my friends. I am also grateful for each day that the Lord has given to me as if it is a gift, a present. No one knows what tomorrow holds. We take our life for granted but know that our health can be taken away at any time. Life is good and my prayer now is when my time comes to be with God I will be able to say like Paul, "I have finished the race, I have kept the good fight of faith. (2Tim 4:7).

Thank You,
Liz Orr

My Assignment

Have you ever thought about your purpose on earth? I have thought about it a lot and have been asking God what He wants me to do with the rest of my life? First of all we are called to bring glory to God on this Earth.

Most of the time we are waiting for some big thing to do but my assignment is quite simple. My assignment is just to live and let others know that they can live too. In spite of stage IV cancer God has allowed me to live and to give Him the glory with my life.

There is nothing too hard for God that he can't heal or deliver you from. Yes the cancer is still in my body but until God heals me completely from it, I am to live life to the fullest with a smile and let others know that God loves us in spite of what life brings us. You know the saying, "if life brings you lemons, make lemonade." I thank God for my assignment and I know there are others out there whose assignments are just to live and give God the glory....

Jesus said in John 17:4, "I have brought you glory on Earth by completing the work you have given me to do."

It's In The Valleys I Grow

Sometimes life seems hard to bear,
Full of sorrow, trouble and woe
It's then I have to remember
That it's in the valleys I grow.

If I always stayed on the mountain top
And never experienced pain,
I would never appreciate God's love
And would be living in vain.

I have so much to learn
And my growth is very slow,
Sometimes I need the mountain tops,
But it's in the valleys I grow.

I do not always understand
Why things happen as they do,
But I am very sure of one thing.
My Lord will see me through.

My little valleys are nothing
When I picture Christ on the cross
He went through the valley of death;
His victory was Satan's loss.

Forgive me Lord, for complaining
When I'm feeling so very low.
Just give me a gentle reminder
That it's in the valleys I grow.

Continue to strengthen me, Lord
And use my life each day
To share your love with others
And help them find their way.
Thank you for valleys, Lord
For this one thing I know
The mountain tops are glorious
But it's in the valleys I grow!

Author - Jane Eggleston

Archie's Tribute

So why I am here? It's quite simple. It is because of Mrs. Liz. I think it is important to tell you a little bit of how I know Mrs. Liz.

In late 2002, Le Creuset had grown and the finance department needed help so we ran a help wanted ad. I found a draft of the ad we would run and it simply read that Le Creuset seeked a full-charge bookkeeper to perform general accounting duties in the daily administration of the accounting process. Record/reconcile sales data, analyzes accounts, performs bank reconciliations, and assists with governmental reporting; assists the Retail Accounting manager as needed. Little did I know what was in store when we placed that ad.

The ad should have said Le Creuset requires a special kind of employee. This employee will be intelligent, honest, hard working, dedicated, and strong willed. She will listen to you when she needs to but she will also question you when she needs to. She will not always like the computers and she will be frustrated like employees will be with the deadlines and the volume of work. However, she will bring heart to the company and you will be all the better for it.

While she will need to be trained, so will you. I have the perfect employee....Liz Orr.

So I was fortunate enough to interview Mrs. Liz and hire her into the accounting department....and we worked happily ever after. WRONG!!! A lot of you may experience this but even though we work for one company, each department and even sections in that department have their unique challenges. It was through those shared challenges and experiences that Mrs. Liz and I became friends. Was it always easy? No. We had our good times and we had our bad times. As you work with each other you and spend time with each other you learn their personality.....you know when to push and when to step back. The crazy and fascinating thing about our jobs was that pretty much each day held a challenge of some sort. We were defiantly not bored. I taught Mrs. Liz some things about computers and accounting, while she taught me (even though I didn't always listen) about how to be a supervisor. We always had to deal with a lot of information, so I would on occasion try to improve things and change things by introducing a new procedure. I will give Mrs. Liz credit....she trusted me and she worked with me (kicking a screaming at times) to make these improvements. Everything did not worked as planned but we tried. I think we ran into problems some times and when she would come to me to fix something and I was hoping she would know what to do because I sure didn't. But we worked through it.

I mentioned earlier that Mrs. Liz has brought heart to the company and I really do mean that. People often say that we spend more time with our co-workers than family and it's true some times. When you work with people a while, you actually share a lot of yourself. You share in joy and sorrow….you share in their life. With Mrs. Liz it was no different. I can't think of many days when Mrs. Liz didn't come through the office saying "Happy Monday!!" on a Monday or "Happy Tuesday" on Tuesdays etc….when we were all just look forward to "Happy Friday". Mrs. Liz was there actually there cheering us through each day.

Part of Mrs. Liz's involvement with her co-workers was to occasionally give out Birthday cards or get a group together to sing Happy Birthday to someone. Sometimes I would be sitting at my desk and I would see a group of ladies gather together and head off in one direction or another. Call me paranoid but I get nervous when I see a small mob form. It was always great to see and hear the ladies choir "perform" for their friends. A card and song…we often take for granted how much they mean. But equally important is to be there when someone needs to talk to someone or when they have lost a loved one and Mrs. Liz was there….either with a sympathy card or shoulder to lean on.

In May of last year things changed. Next we heard she had cancer…. next that she was taking treatments….and next that more treatments were needed. Some of the hardest things we had to do at work were to fill Mrs. Liz's position and see her clean out her office.

Don't be sad because the story does not end there. While Mrs. Liz does not work with us on a daily basis she is still part of our dysfunctional family. Mrs. Liz does stop by on occasion and I shared with her in an email during Christmas what I see when she does. I see friendship, care, and concern. I see her greeted with genuine smiles and hugs and I see the support she has. There are even people in France that ask about her and one sent a card to let her know that she was thinking about her….

But why did this have to happen in the first place? It is said that Mother Teresa once said when reminded that God does not give us any burdens we cannot handle that she replied "I know, but sometimes I just wish He didn't think so highly of me."

When you hear of someone with cancer you often hear they are "fighting" cancer and they have "rounds" of treatments. It sounds a lot like a boxing match with Mrs. Liz in a ring fighting this "thing". When you are hit look to back to your corner and see what is there. A strong faith and a lot of friends yelling "Don't give up" and "You can do it".

Mrs. Liz your faith and love for the Lord is more than sufficient to see you through this but you have the added benefit of a great family and lot of supportive friends to help you to and I am honored to be one of them.

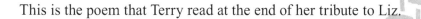

This is the poem that Terry read at the end of her tribute to Liz.

My Sister, My Friend
© Leann Stiegman - Author

To me you are an angel in disguise.
Full of intuition, intelligent, and wise.
Always giving and helping through
Good times and bad.
You are the best friend I've ever had.
If I had one wish it would surely be
to give you as much as you've given to me.
Though we've been through some cloudy days,
you've been my sunshine in so many ways.
Through trials and tests, right by me
you stood, and gave me your hand whenever you could.
Thank you so much my sister, my friend,
my gratitude for you has no end.

Much Love,
Terry Orr-Sander

Terry's Tribute

My Tribute to Liz

A lot happened in the early 80's. I was only 12 years old but I remember quite a bit. Our President was Jimmy Carter; Dallas, the Dukes of Hazard, and the Love Boat were a few of my favorite shows; a walkman was something I wanted to own, but didn't. The Heisman Trophy winner was George Rogers…and my brother brought home a girl from Allendale and they called her Nookie!

Who is this girl? Living in Hampton we all knew we didn't socialize with Allendale folks like that. Was my brother out of his mind???

She was tall…which was kind of intimidating…but I later realized as the family and I got to know her…she spoke with a soft tone, she was beautiful, caring, giving and kind.

The next thing I know….I have a brand new nephew…JAMEL and a Sister-in-law.

As the years passed Nookie turned into Liz….. Liz turned into Evangelist Orr and my sister-in–law turned into my sister and friend.

There are many things I can say about Liz. First in foremost she is a great wife, mother and grandmother. Trust me, it takes someone special like her to be able to deal with all of that testosterone in one house. My brother and nephews love her and know they have a jewel among them. I have realized my brother wasn't out of his mind, but in his right mind when he knew he couldn't live without her.

She genuinely cares about people and shows her love in various ways. Liz is a great encourager. Even on the days I called to be a shoulder for her…she always seemed to have a word for me. I'm sure all of us that are here today have been encouraged by this great woman in some way. Liz has a way of touching people's lives which leaves an everlasting mark on them. She can't help it…God just made her that way.

Liz is intelligent, creative and enjoys staying busy. My brother and I get exhausted just by watching her. She loves numbers and is great at analyzing things. You can give her any meal and she can tell you one by one what ingredient you used to make your so called "secret family recipe." We go shopping and before I can get my calculator out to figure out the discount…she's got it already. So, I decided to just to leave my calculator at home…I don't need it….I got Liz.

Last but not least, one of the best decisions she ever made, besides marrying my handsome brother, and giving birth to my three wonderful nephews, was accepting Christ as her Lord and Personal Savior. God truly changed her life and I know she wouldn't have it any other way. I can remember back in the day when Liz was called a "boot leg minister"…slipping a sermon in during praise and worship. I knew even back then that her calling was great and God would use her mightily for his Kingdom. Evangelist Orr truly loves God and His Word with everything inside of her and she does her best to live her life to demonstrate just that.

Her love for her family and others, seeing her strength during this difficult time, and her passion to serve God in spite of any situation, is an inspiration to me and to all of you that know her.

Liz, on behalf of my sisters and my brother, you have been a blessing to our family and we want you to know that you are loved very much and that we standing with you. REMEMBER: TOUGH TIMES NEVER LAST, BUT TOUGH PEOPLE LIKE YOU DO!

To Liz……

My Sister, My Friend

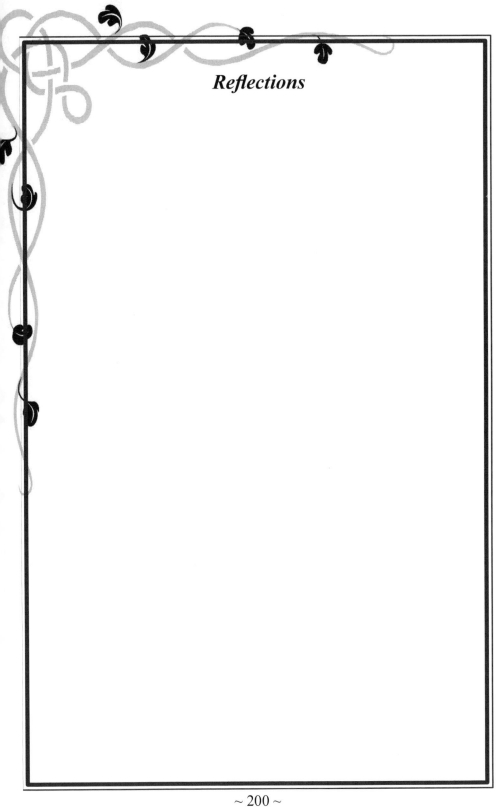

Reflections

Reflections